Jew(ish)

ALSO BY MATT GREENE

Ostrich

Jew(ish)

~~A primer~~ ~~A memoir~~
~~A manual~~ <u>A plea</u>

Matt Greene

Little
a

Published by Little A, Seattle

www.apub.com

Amazon, the Amazon logo, and Little A are trademarks of Amazon.com, Inc.,
or its affiliates.

ISBN-13: 9781542023443
ISBN-10: 1542023440

Cover design by The Brewster Project

Printed in the United States of America

For my family: past, present and future

'I don't deserve this award, but then I have
arthritis and I don't deserve that either'

— Jack Benny

'A Jew without a beard is better than a beard
without a Jew'

— Yiddish proverb

Prologue

On 22 January 2017, around one in the afternoon, I became a parent. By then my partner Imogen had been in labour for almost thirty-six hours. The first ten or so of these hours had gone roughly to plan (our midwife had suggested we write one to ensure we felt in control of the birth when it came). Originally Imogen had wanted a home birth – she and all three of her siblings were born at home, deep in the countryside where the nearest Emergency Unit was several hours away – but some small complications in her bloodwork meant she'd need to have antibiotics administered during the delivery. The amended plan, then, was to remain at home until the last moment then go to a midwife-led suite at the hospital, possibly with a bathtub, if one was available, for the final leg.

The labour had started at four the previous morning and we'd been up since five, lighting candles and gently swaying to British Sea Power. As per the plan I'd made Imogen cheese and tuna toasties, and tea for the midwife who'd arrived at five thirty and parted not long after with some words of encouragement. Everything was going perfectly. We should get some rest and call her again when the contractions were a minute apart.

By eleven o'clock we were in an Uber on our way to the hospital, making small talk with a driver spectacularly incapable of reading a room. I'd called our delightful Welsh midwife when the contractions had sped up and had the kettle on in readiness for a resumption of a discussion on her past life as an actor, but by 10.23 we were gathered in silence at the foot of our bed. Imogen was in it, looking anxious, and the midwife was over her, stethoscope in hand, looking anxiouser. She was struggling to hear a heartbeat.

In the hospital, after a torturous period of waiting for a bed to become free, we were hurried through to the fluorescent-lit ward where Imogen was clamped to a bed and attached to a barrage of drips and monitors. Through one we could hear a faint heartbeat, an irregular, aquatic *whomp* that grew quieter and more skittish as the contractions intensified. A nurse was explaining something without the benefit of a soothing Welsh lilt when suddenly a button was pressed and within seconds the room was flooded with people in masks: nurses, doctors, anaesthetists. Imogen looked up at me and squeezed my hand like a collapsing star. The most fearless person I know was afraid.

A month earlier I'd fielded a call from my dad. I was working on the umpteenth draft of a failing novel about contemporary Jewish identity and the legacy of the Holocaust in secular Jewish life and was grateful for the distraction. We talked about the previous night's football game, work, as much politics as we could mutually stomach, then a pause bled down the line. My father and I have always been close – as I said in a toast at his wedding, he's been like a father to me – and I knew at once what the pause augured: we were about to broach a Difficult Subject. At the pause's edge he dived straight in – this is a man who sends emails with blank bodies, the entire content contained within the subject line. 'There're two things we need to discuss,' he told me. 'First thing, what are you thinking re circumcision?'

'What's the second thing?' I asked.

'Your grandfather's Hebrew name was *Yehoshua*. I thought you'd want to know.'

'. . .'

'It would mean a lot to me if you could include it somewhere in the name.'

We had a name. It was the product of many months' discussion. I told him so.

Another pause. In negotiations my dad can use silence like a game of chicken. He's good at negotiating. His whole career has been based on it. Sure enough I expanded to fill it.

I tried to explain that Imogen had family too, that the child would be getting our family name (his father's surname), which was no small thing, that Imogen also had beloved grandparents who were no longer with us.

The line fell quiet. 'And I suppose it's a no to circumcision too?'

'. . .'

'It wouldn't have to be a ceremony. You could do it in a hospital with a medical professional, not at home with an audience and a buffet.'

Again, I said nothing. 'I'm saying nothing,' I said.

'Well, as long as you've thought it through.'

'I have,' I lied. 'If it's something he wants he can do it when he's older.'

Dad scoffed. 'Would *you*?'

Well, no. And wasn't that the point? Imogen and I had discussed it only as long as it had taken to confirm the assumption that we agreed. Circumcision was a barbaric, probably traumatising, practice. I still couldn't eat calamari without crossing my legs.

I didn't say this to my dad, though. Instead, feeling proud of myself for my maturity and magnanimity, I extended a peace offering. 'I'm glad you brought up Grandpa's Hebrew name because we wanted him to have one and I was meaning to ask—'

Dad cut me off, not cruelly but curtly. 'Well, if you're not going to get him circumcised what's the bloody point in giving him a Hebrew name?'

3

Back in the hospital ward I'd been handed scrubs and a too-young-looking nurse was swabbing at Imogen's arm. There was too much talking to hear the monitors but behind her I could read the line on the display. I have no medical training – I've never even seen *ER* – but I could see it wasn't good. The staff were talking over us, a dozen voices webbing above our heads, shouting numbers, barking instructions. I gripped Imogen's hand and told her it was fine. A contraction rolled across her. An alarm sounded. A hundred possible futures unspooled before me, not one of them good. This was the thing we'd never come back from. At just that moment the heartrate returned, distant but steady. It took the doctors a moment to notice but as soon as one did the panic sucked from the room. Voices returned to their regular pitch. It felt almost like disappointment.

Slowly, like a Marx Brothers sketch in reverse, the room emptied till it was just Imogen, me and the trainee midwife assigned to her observation. Just the four of us. In the long hours that followed, scored by those faint *whomp*s which would stop for seconds at a time, I wish I could say it occurred to me to pray but the thought never crossed my mind; I hadn't seen the inside of a synagogue since the previous millennium and even then it would never have occurred to me to pray in one – as my mum once explained, she didn't go to synagogue to be with God, she went to be with people. I have a friend who's always striking deals with a god he neither trusts nor believes in, little sacrifices he hopes might serve as leverage towards some greater benefit: a United loss here for the next round in a job interview, a rejected submission for an all-clear on a health scare. This is the only view of prayer I've ever been able to countenance: a negotiation in which the goal is to remain silent for longer than your opponent (God).

I had nothing to offer of appropriate value, and I wasn't a non-practising Jew, I was no Jew at all. Rather, any sense of Jewishness

I had held on to had nothing to do with even a vestigial belief in some higher power whose benevolence I could appeal to. Jewishness wasn't something I could turn to in a moment of need. If it was anything at all, it was more like an outlook. It was a filter. It was an inflection. A sensibility. A set of shared cultural assumptions. It was . . . It was complicated.

At three on Saturday morning, after a whole day of labour, Imogen was offered an epidural and stood stock-still, mid-contraction, as a needle the size of a bike pump was inserted at the base of her spine. And at one o'clock that afternoon, just before the midwife's lunchbreak, our son, Arthur, was born.

The first time I held him, and in the hours and days that followed, I didn't think once about foreskin or forenames, Jewish or otherwise. I was too in love for the world to be a part of it. Not just with Arthur but with Imogen, my incredible partner who'd given us this miracle. If childbirth is a miracle, it's a miracle of courage, of will and of science – and for second children, a miracle of forgetting – and in those first days I couldn't look at him without my feelings of gratitude and awe overwhelming me.

Just two days before Arthur's birth I'd sat rocking in front of my laptop as a racist sock puppet was inaugurated into the highest office in Western politics, an office he'd won by courting conspiracy theorists and white supremacists. For the past few years I'd sat rocking in front of the same computer, trying to write jokes but mostly just gawping at the decay of Western liberalism, watching with a growing knot of unease as our politics devolved into the language of difference and refugees became migrants became numbers became waves. But for now the world was a distant argument I had no stake in, a TV blaring on the other side of a concrete wall.

Slowly, though, life comes back, altered but recognisable and familiar in its relentlessness. When you're looking after small children you get lots of time to think – not for much else – and over the course of those next few weeks I found my thoughts returning, tentatively at first but with growing insistence, to the question of my Jewishness.

Having a child means many things, most of which I'm still yet to discover, but one of them is explaining the world to someone encountering it for the first time, and this requires understanding, at the very least, your place within it. Perhaps that's why it forces you to ask the questions that might have seemed less urgent before you had kids.

The year 2020 is a strange time to be a Jew, even, or perhaps especially, a lapsed, secular one. At once we're witnessing a resurgence of the far right, an uptick in anti-Semitic attacks, a refugee crisis of a scale unknown since the Second World War and, maybe most crucially for the question this book primarily concerns itself with, the end of the generation who witnessed the horrors of the Holocaust first-hand. In this context it seems important to understand what it means to be Jewish – and personally what it means to me that, technically, my son is not. There are chapters in this book about several key aspects of modern Jewish experience. There's one about God, one about comedy, one about my family history, one about the internet, and, unavoidably, essays about Israel and the Holocaust that include an account of a trip I took to Poland on my last birthday, to the place my relatives were most likely murdered.

In writing them I hoped to understand the ways in which being Jewish, something that for a long time I considered peripheral to my sense of self, has informed my world view, shaped my life, and influenced the company I keep and the choices I continue to make. I wanted to explore what it means to be defined by an identity you may have personally rejected, one I continue to struggle with, and one that increasingly struggles with me. There is a chapter in here that aims to explain how some Jews in some communities view Jews like me as the greatest existential threat our people have ever

6

faced. I also hoped to explain why 2020 is such a difficult time to be a Jew, religious or otherwise, what it means that the Holocaust is passing from lived experience to collective memory, and why rising anti-Semitism on both sides of the Atlantic has many Jews fearing for their communities' futures. Most of all I hoped to give a sense of what it feels like to be, if not a Jew, then at least Jew*ish*.

These chapters contain everything that thirty-four years have taught me about being Jewish, and everything being Jewish has taught me about living in a world that, in the words of my favourite non-Jewish satirist Peter Cook, has learned from its mistakes and seems confident it can replicate them exactly. I hope they might expand on some of the clichés you're familiar with, introduce you to some new ones, and most of all, give you some insight into what we might very loosely call the contemporary Jewish experience.

Chapter One:
God

I was seven years old when I realised I was Jewish. To be more precise, I was seven years old when I realised not everyone was Jewish. It happened at my friend Arun's house. It's always strange visiting friends' houses when you're a kid. The food is different, the temperature is different, there's a different shoe policy, people talk to each other differently. Since, at seven, your home is at least three quarters of your world, all of these differences are jarring, like errors someone should have caught and eliminated. But Arun's house was even more different than my friend Josh's or my friend Daniel's. There was a sliding door before the proper front door with an area between them that was neither outside nor in; pots of herbs flourished on the windowsills; there was fruit without stickers on it in plastic baskets; little gold trinkets on the sideboards and mantelpieces; and rich, alluring smells wafting from the kitchen. (Years later I would learn this was called *flavour*.)

Most jarring of all, however, was the shrine above the fireplace in the living room where we settled in the deep shag to draw or play Top Trumps. In frames, like certificates or photos of relatives, were paintings of multi-limbed creatures – part-human, part-animal – sitting cross-legged in flowers or smiling from plinths with exotic fruits held aloft on silver trays. Around these pictures stood carvings of the same figures, candles, pink and white blossoms, and copper bowls that in our house would be spilling with car keys or loose change. What struck me as most different, perhaps, was the jewellery the creatures were adorned with: sparkling gold bracelets, ornate jewelled crowns and dangling earrings that looked like miniature antique birdcages. And then there were the smiles. Those smiles. Calming, benevolent, beatific.

No one I knew would dream of letting a god into their home. Sure, we had *mezuzahs* (a kind of ornament that contains a page of the Torah) on our door frames, and once a week we lit candles and said three prayers, but who in their right mind would invite a stranger into the place that they slept? Even in *shul* (synagogue) no one talked about God, or if they did it was in Hebrew, which didn't count since no one knew what it meant. Instead the rabbi would talk about adult things: charity appeals and respecting our parents. Years later, I'd think of this while watching Peter Sellers as President Merkin Muffley in *Dr. Strangelove*. 'Gentlemen, you can't fight in here, this is the War Room!'

I don't remember my parents using God as an easy out when they were sick of answering our questions about why the sky was blue or why only men had moustaches. ('Because God said so.') Neither did they involve him in arbitration. Why did we have to go to school, brush our teeth, clean our bedrooms, rinse the water jug with water when that was all it had in it?

And they could've.

Because the Jewish God was a vengeful God. For us there were no trays of fruit or benevolent smiles; there wasn't a physical form at all. God was everywhere and by extension nowhere. He was like big data or CCTV. The difference between the Jewish God and the Christian God that the majority of classmates never talked about and weren't expected to believe in, was like the difference between a Hollywood blockbuster and the European arthouse short it was based on.[1] Everything about the New Testament, from the L'Oréal locks of its leading man (the original pin-up in more ways than one) to the third-act reversal of the resurrection, smacked of a story written by committee with all eyes on the box office receipts.

By contrast, the Jewish God scored low for likeability. He was cruel and capricious. He wouldn't forgive a blind man for not polishing his shoes. Once a year, at Passover, we gathered as a family and thanked Him for freeing us from bondage in Egypt. As part of our escape, to teach our captors a lesson, He'd killed all their firstborn sons, just as the Egyptians had ordered the murder of their slaves' firstborn sons. Each year we sang a song of praise for this. It was called *Dayenu*, which means *It would've been enough*. If He'd only taken us from slavery – *dayenu*. If He'd only drowned our enemies – *dayenu*. It didn't feel like we were thanking Him for saving us, more holding Him back, pleading with Him to maybe next time consider some diplomatic channels.

The Jewish God was an enforcer. A Roy Keane figure. Less Al Pacino in *The Godfather* than Al Pacino in *The Godfather II*. He was a fearsome older brother who might protect you on the playground but would terrorise you doubly as soon as you got home. He wasn't a safety net or the promise of a warm bed at the end of a long day. He was the reason you slept with one eye open.

But all of this I learned later, in Sunday school, since God was not one of my parents' acquaintances. He was entirely absent from

---

1 Jews are the original hipsters, which is perhaps one reason so many people hate us so much.

11

our home, and not absent in a way that drew attention to itself. Not absent like a father. Absent like an absence.

There are as many types of Jew as there are fillings for bagels, but one thing we perhaps all have in common is that we each consider ourselves either more or less observant than we are. There are Jews who go to shul every day, those who go every week, those who go once a year on Yom Kippur and those who don't go at all. No one type is more or less Jewish than the next, although certainly some might dispute that, and in some senses it's the most religious who have least to consider in terms of what constitutes their Jewish identity.

In our case, though, the confusion didn't arise so much from God's absence in our everyday life as from his absence from the things we did in His honour. Once a week, on a Friday night, like many Jewish families, we gathered round the table in the kitchen and made kiddush to usher in Shabbat, the Jewish Sabbath. This was the one time each week we'd have looked conspicuously Jewish to even the most casual observer. The men (my dad, my brother and I) wore skullcaps fastened with metal clips, and the women (my mum and my two sisters) lit two tall white candles in silver holders, waving their hands like bored masseurs as the flames flickered beneath. Next we said blessings for the bread – a plaited, brioche-like substance called *challah* – for the wine,[2] and on washing our hands, which, to the confusion of the guests we occasionally invited, we mimed. My dad, looking studiously at the text but reciting from memory, said a few lines in Hebrew, and finally (the whole 'service' took less than five minutes but seemed to last forever, standing as it did in the way of the food) my mum presented dinner, the same each week: chicken soup then roast chicken, with fruit for dessert.

---

2   In an episode of *Frasier* where Frasier and Niles have to pretend to be Jewish, their first act is to dump several pounds of sugar into a carafe of red. 'Dreadful!' exclaims Frasier on trying it. 'Perfect,' Niles retorts.

All of this bore the hallmarks of religious practice – the deference, the repetition, the flames – but there was one crucial difference: no belief underpinned it. If God had dropped by to borrow a tyre iron or establish an alibi, we'd have flicked Him an eyebrow then gone back to arguing over our positions on the sofa for *Have I Got News For You*.

Similarly, when I was caught sneaking chocolates from the cupboards or sweets from the sweet shop, God formed no part of the reprimand. I couldn't eat Chewits because they were made with gelatine, which came from pigs' bones, and I couldn't eat chocolate for three hours after meals because it was against the rules of kashrut – the law that decides which foods are kosher and which foods aren't. And what did that have to do with believing in God? You didn't have to believe in Him to respect his decrees. You didn't even have to mention His name.

Unlike the tooth fairy or trickle-down economics, neither of my parents even pretended to believe in God, but still it was a surprise when I asked them outright. I don't know what I expected – perhaps a telling-off or some dull theological lecture. Maybe even proof. But what I got confirmed a growing suspicion: that for all our practice, we were Jewish in name only. Mum panicked, turning red and jabbering something about the capacity for human kindness or a shiver of breeze on the surface of a lake, while Dad smiled ruefully and told my sisters, who duly obliged, to cover their ears. This, inevitably, was a Friday-night dinner, where all of our discussions took place. The sun had set, making mirrors of the glass doors that gave on to the garden, and in their reflection I could see the whole scene play out in the third person, the person that holds most of my memories.

Dad smiled some more. 'I believe in the power of belief,' he answered eventually, talking slowly, carefully, as if from a prepared statement, like he was drawing water from a well. 'If enough people believe the market's going to crash, the market'll crash.'

I had no idea what this meant, let alone what it had to do with my question.

'Belief is like in the cartoon when the Roadrunner runs over the cliff edge,' he went on. 'He's fine so long as he doesn't look down. Belief is important. It's real. And I fully believe in everyone's right to believe in whatever it is they choose to believe in.'

I waited again. But apparently this was his answer in full.

'So no?'

My older brother, who'd been through this the previous year, rolled his eyes and Dad turned to my sisters and told them to hum a song. They obliged. Probably something by Crowded House or Destiny's Child.

'It doesn't matter whether I do or I don't,' he told me. 'God's not important. What's important is community. Just because you don't believe in God doesn't mean you don't have to go to shul.'

'But that's ridiculous. You wouldn't go to the cinema if you didn't think there was a projectionist.' It's possible I'm misremembering the extent of my pre-teen eloquence.

'It depends who you went with,' said my dad, responding seamlessly to the analogy I'd made twenty years in the future. 'Just because I don't believe there's a man in the sky with a beard and a staff who dispenses judgements and writes rules on bricks doesn't mean I don't have obligations.'

'So you admit it, you don't!'

He shrugged. 'There's nothing to admit. I'm simply stating a position. You shouldn't ask a question if you're not prepared for the answer.'

And yet, confusingly (to me at least), by any objective gauge you could care to pick, we were religious. We weren't *frum*, a word we used only disparagingly in reference to the black-hatted *frummers* we saw on the Northern line, or trudging up the side of the A41 on Saturday afternoons with their clunky shoes and waterslide sideburns, but even compared to the majority of my friends we were observant.[3] We had mezuzahs on each door, a drawer full of *siddurs* (prayer books) and *kippahs* (skullcaps) and two sets of cutlery and crockery (one for meat and one for milk). In the run-up to Passover, my mum would clean the house so thoroughly the floors got lower, then she would bring out a third set of cutlery, which was kept in storage for the rest of the year so that not one risen crumb would ever touch it.

But while we took all this seriously and followed these rules like something depended on it, we were also on a constant lookout for loopholes. Judaism was like a coupon scheme: if you were thorough and knew where to look there were always savings to be made. For example, kashrut forbids cooking a beast in the milk of its mother, but at restaurants it was fine to have cheese on your burger or parmesan on bolognaise. By extension, takeaways couldn't contain meat at all and, as a precaution, were eaten in the garden – which was one of God's many blind spots. Invariably this led to dispute: my brother straddling the lintel of the door in the kitchen, one foot inside, one foot out, while my mum implored him, in the slow, steady voice of a fireman talking a jumper down from his ledge, to for the love of God lower the Big Mac. Most revealing of all, it was forbidden to write the word *God* – this for Jews was considered sacrilege – but it was permitted to write the word *G–d*. As if He were winking up at you, co-conspirator in the trick you'd just pulled.

That Jews aren't really a race is an argument beloved by racists and anti-Semites alike, but a rarer, adjacent truth is that Judaism isn't really a religion. You might think it's semantics but I'd argue it's mechanics. Look under the bonnet of most major

---

3   Jews are never *practising*, *devout* or *religious* (or *unreligious*) but *observant*, like private detectives or a Neighbourhood Watch scheme.

religions and you'll find a system of beliefs that's at least internally consistent (the clue's in the name: they're *faiths*). But the engine for Judaism isn't faith. It's doubt. What keeps the vehicle moving isn't the belief that it *will* but the heat generated from a thousand simultaneous disagreements. This might sound glib or pedantic but it's evident in one of Judaism's most foundational facts. Our most sacred text isn't the Torah, the purported word of Hashem, but the Talmud, a multi-volume companion text that interprets, expands and comments. Essentially the Talmud is marginalia, a conversation. A beneath-the-line comments section. What Judaism essentially amounts to is a four-thousand-year-old argument.

But Judaism is easier to define than Jewishness, which is what interests me more. Growing up, what it mostly felt like was a punishment. Being Jewish, as far as I could tell, was like being grounded. It consisted of an endless series of prohibitions. Not only could we not eat sweets or cheeseburgers, we couldn't go out on Friday nights or lie in on Sunday mornings, since that was for *cheder* (Hebrew school), where we learned that teachers who had no training as teachers were unable to control classrooms full of bored pre-teens experimenting with rebellion.

And then there was Christmas: not just a day in a calendar but the arc towards which the whole year bent. The feelings of loss and estrangement would begin in September, when the nights drew in and the air filled with the almond scent of freshly laid tarmac. Christmas was the trade-off for the ending of summer and the curtailment of freedoms this comprised. Classmates would make lists and talk excitedly of plans for holidays and gatherings.

In November, when the ads came out, they'd tear pages from catalogues and pass them like contraband under desks, and before long they'd be drafting their letters to Santa, who, no matter how loudly we shouted about his suspect diet and unethical work practices, never dimmed in their imaginations. But if the build-up was torture, the day itself was unbearable.

We lived in a house off a motorway exit ramp – the suburbs of suburbia – in a village with no high street and one bus stop, our nearest neighbours too far away for us to hear their sleigh bells and the rips of their wrapping paper. We didn't watch TV (that rare prohibition that had nothing to do with religion but was rather something my parents actually believed in), and my siblings and I were too young to own radios or read papers. Christmas, then, wasn't acknowledged at all. Most years we'd wake up on Boxing Day as if from a collective coma, unaware that we'd even missed it. Once, my mum made a coincidental turkey curry, a dish that wasn't part of her repertoire (Fifty Things To Do With Leftover Chicken), and that never appeared again.

Another time, to escape the near-fatal ennui, we went away on a ski trip to the Alps. On the first morning I broke my leg and spent the rest of the holiday in a cast. Taking pity, my mum bequeathed me a pocketful of shiny francs and suggested I take myself to a games arcade we'd seen in the town while hiring our boots. Painfully, I negotiated a perilous gauntlet of black ice and grey snow with cars speeding on one side and a sheer drop on the other, earning blisters on my palms and probable frostbite in my cast-encased toes, only to find that the arcade was closed. Not just that, the whole town was closed. Not a door was unlocked nor shutter unshuttered, and of course there were no buses to take me back up the mountain. It was only days later that I realised why.

'But look,' you'll say, as so many have, 'it's all well and good feeling sorry for yourself, but there must've been compensations. It can't all have been bad. Didn't you have Chanukah instead?'

This is what everyone asks when you tell them you've never celebrated Christmas. Never drunk eggnog or watched *Die Hard*. Chanukah, or 'Jewish Christmas' as it's dubbed by people who know no better and those with a cruel sense of irony, is a minor festival that happens occasionally to coincide with Christmas.[4] The story of Chanukah centres on the Maccabees, leaders of a Jewish rebel army, and an against-the-odds victory over the forces of the mad Syrian king Antiochus that nevertheless saw them holed up in a temple with only enough oil to burn a candle for a day. The miracle from which the festival derives is that the oil, in fact, burned for eight days until more oil was found. Or to put it another way: some oil that we thought would last for a short bit of time lasted for a slightly longer but still quite short time. Essentially, Chanukah is a festival in honour of the time your mobile ran Waze from Margate to Brighton on only 20 per cent battery. The miracle is resource management, and our celebrations reflected this moral. Technically eight days of Chanukah meant eight days of presents, but in truth it meant one present with a seven-day publicity campaign. This didn't do much for our sense of wonder and surprise. If on day one you got the batteries, on day four you knew to expect the torch. If on day one it was a sock, on day three it was the pair. One year, I swear I got a sweater on the eighth day and on the seventh the receipt. In Finland, or wherever he lives, Father Christmas wasn't losing any sleep.

As well as Chanukah we had Rosh Hashanah, Purim, Tu Bishvat, Shavuot and, of course, Passover. This was the big one.

---

4   Rather than the Gregorian calendar, Jewish festivals are dispersed across a lunisolar one that has no other function. See footnote 1.

For a whole week we were banned from eating anything leavened in remembrance of our ancestors' flight from Egypt, during which there'd been no time for our bread to rise, so presumably they too had spent a week eating crackers and the next fortnight drinking prune juice.

The festival commemorated their enslavement in Ancient Egypt. (One stereotype about Jewish people is that we're bad at manual work, but who do you think built the pyramids?) Finally, we'd been rescued by Moses and God at His most Charles Bronson, the latter unleashing a storm of plagues upon our Egyptian oppressors. Later, after forty years in the desert, Moses was banned from the Holy Land for kicking a rock, but earlier in his career he was a highly rated young saviour with a wand of a left foot, who'd been hidden in a basket and set afloat on a river to save him from slaughter, surviving only when he was stranded in some bullrushes and brought up as an Egyptian. Eventually, as with all Jewish stories, he'd grown into a fearless revolutionary and laid waste the shackles of oppression that had held his people in bondage for as long as anyone could remember.

To celebrate all of this we gathered round the kitchen table, which was really now two tables – our regular table and a round one from the garage that sat at its foot like a point in an exclamation – and told this story in painstaking detail, pausing only to recharge our glasses, since what this service amounted to was the world's slowest and most depressing drinking game. We drank wine to commemorate our enslavement, to commemorate our punishment by the Egyptians, to commemorate the punishment of the Egyptians by God . . . And all of this on an empty stomach, since for the first few hours the only food on the table was symbolic: bitter herbs to represent the bitterness of our ancestors' years of enslavement; salt water to represent their tears; a roasted egg, which had something to do with mourning; and a lamb bone to symbolise the lamb we'd slaughtered so we could daub its blood on our doors so that the Angel of Death would 'pass over' our houses on his mission of revenge. Finally we took a break from *our* Exodus (the pronoun was important: you had to imagine it had happened to you) to answer the Questions of the Four Children.

The Four Children were the four types of children delineated in the Torah. Since I had three siblings, the casting was always a source of amusement. There was the Wise Child, my older brother Daniel, who ruled with an iron fist in an iron glove and took the title to heart; the Simple Child, my sister Rachel, who was everyone's favourite;[5] the Child Who Is Too Young To Ask, my other sister Hannah, who had the misfortune of being the youngest. And then there was the Wicked Child. That was me. The question I had to ask was less a question than a pose I had to strike, one that stuck for the next twenty or so years:

What is this service of yours? Why do you bother?[6]

The Torah was firm in its suggestion for how this type of child be treated. My parents, the leaders of the service, should *blunt my teeth.*

Because he doesn't want to be a part of us, he proves he does not believe in the Torah, so you must answer him sharply. Tell him that it is because of these mitzvot *that Hashem did miracles for me when I left Egypt. You must stress for me, and not for people like him. If the Wicked Child were in Egypt, he would not have been saved.*

All of which seemed ludicrously unfair considering what I thought I knew about how Judaism worked. Was I really to be left

---

5   Perhaps the funniest and most brutal story in my family's lore is the time my grandfather, on his deathbed, beckoned our other sister closer and told her this, having mistaken her for Rachel. He realised moments later and died the next day from embarrassment.

6   To understand Jews you need to look at the pronouns.

to hang for the crime of asking a question? Was Judaism no better than a teacher who dismisses a bored pupil rather than work harder to engage them in the subject? And what was so wise about the Wise Child, whose 'question', the softest of softball lobs, wasn't a question at all but a sycophantic reverie, a piece of gutless ingratiation: *Oh please, tell me more about these customs!*

And besides, wasn't Jewishness less about being a part of something than apart from it? Wasn't the lesson of the Talmud to think for yourself and, by extension, to be wary of doctrine and groupthink and the identities they forged?

Apparently not.

And then there was Yom Kippur, the day of atonement, where we were forbidden from eating or drinking anything at all, leaven or otherwise, for twenty-five hours (because any old schmo could manage twenty-four). This prohibition apparently extended to toothpaste and since this was the one time of year I actually went to shul, my strongest association with Judaism, and Jewishness by extension, was halitosis.

By the age of thirteen, after a decade of playing the Wicked Child, I'd taken the title to heart and begun to rebel in earnest. My friend Dave and I would sneak back to his, stalking the empty streets, to play Mario Kart and help ourselves to slices of chocolate cake from his parents' walk-in fridge. The guilt was immediate and settled like a fog, especially when I'd return home to break the fast with my beleaguered family, but it seemed preferable to being a hypocrite, which is what surely I'd have been to participate in a ritual I didn't believe in. Wouldn't that have cheapened it for everyone? And what had I done so wrong that I needed to atone? Asking forgiveness is hardest on the righteous. Besides, what was one more day of deprivation in a life made up of it?

By now I had plenty of non-Jewish friends, friends who for Lent gave up Mars Bar ice creams or pickled onion Monster Munch. Friends who for Christmas got consoles not consolations. And I had Jewish friends who celebrated Christmas. Hindus as well. Sikhs who sought Easter eggs. Muslims who made merry. All of them ate Chewits and, with the exception of the Muslims, enjoyed their foreskins. It was only our family that refused to assimilate to the country we'd lived in since long before my parents were born; a refusal which meant we missed out on the best of everything. Yom Kippur was just an extreme example of the self-denial that shadowed the whole year and that my parents used to stifle my expression and quietly oppress every waking hour of my existence. And *I* was the one meant to be asking forgiveness?

It would be great to say that all of this asceticism was character-building, that it better prepared me for the world of school and friendship in the way a religion surely must if it's to retain any relevance, but truthfully it just sucked. I hated being Jewish in the way I hated being short. There seemed to be no advantage to be gained. There is a reason it's so hard to convert to Judaism: anyone who wants to, by definition, has proven they don't know what it means.

Being Jewish, as far as I could tell, meant feeling left out even, or perhaps especially, when you appeared to fit in. This was maybe the cruellest part: that at first or even second glance no one knew we were any different. In brief, being Jewish was to live a strange double life. We walked through the world with a secret so mundane it was barely worth keeping: our fridges were less interestingly stocked; our holidays lasted longer and were less like holidays; our crockery was segregated, and so too were our schools, cemeteries and dinner tables. Being Jewish was a Ponzi scheme from which no one profited; a shrinking window on a world that had long since outgrown it. It was making the world smaller just when it was opening its arms in acceptance. Digging a moat round your heart and pulling up the drawbridge. There was no part of being Jewish that struck me as beneficial. And that was before I'd even heard the word *anti-Semitism*. Before I learned that Hashem was not the only H word, and certainly not the loudest.

Chapter Two:
Family

When I was thirteen years old my mum's dad, Nat, took me to watch the film *Plunkett & Macleane* at Vue Garston. The film, which for reasons that have long since escaped me I was desperate to see, had a fifteen certificate and I'd consented to the teenage ignominy of being seen in public with a blood relation only because my grandfather had assured me, and my parents, that he'd be able to get me in: just leave it to him. The plan, as far as I can tell, was that the ticket-tearer (probably a teenager himself) would be so awed by my grandpa's seniority that any questions he might have about my age would dissolve in the face of it. In retrospect – as indeed in spect – this was a terrible plan.

Rather than taking an average of our ages, the ticket-tearer took one look at the pre-pubescent teen with his diminutive grandpa and demanded to see some ID. And now my grandpa's show began. The Academy, in its occasional wisdom, overlooked Robert Carlyle and Jonny Lee Miller in the 1999 Oscars for their titular roles in a film Rotten Tomatoes describes as one hundred minutes long, but had a camera been rolling in the foyer of the Vue Garston that day then my grandpa Nat would surely have earned nominations for any category it qualified him in. Among the claims he made was that I was eighteen years old and had a degenerative hormone deficiency and, the pièce de résistance: 'I fought in a war for this country and this is the thanks I get!'

It was this last claim that secured us the partial but pyrrhic victory of a free jumbo vat of popcorn. Back out in the car park, ejected and dejected, buttery and embarrassed, I was naive enough to ask: Was it true? Had he really fought in a war?

My grandpa, never one to let reality get in the way of a principle, flashed a schoolboy smile before reverting to righteous indignation: 'No. But he didn't know that.'

Neither did I. In fact, I knew nothing about my grandfather's background beyond the fact he'd grown up in the East End and used to own a shoe shop, and that his language – often coarse – was peppered with bits of Yiddish, a language that, from my exposure to it, comprised entirely of insults and amusingly abusive directives. *Bang your head on the wall. Go threaten the geese.*

In his house in Stanmore, on top of the piano neither he nor my grandma Helen played, was a photo of my great-grandfather, a man I knew only as *Zeyde* (the Yiddish word for grandfather). Zeyde was Nat's dad, and in the picture, the only one I've ever seen of him, he is leaning across a table at what looks like a black-tie function. His wife, *Bubba* (grandmother), is beside him. The ballroom lighting glints off the frame of his Corrado Soprano glasses and the expression on his face makes him look like he's straining to read a specials board or the bottom line of a bus timetable, lips slightly parted like he's doing so out loud. He looks old in the way people in old photos always look old, even children; like the camera itself isn't positioned in their present but in the future you're now observing them from. It's the sort of photo (you know the ones) that makes people like me, who have no real sense of what it means, automatically reach for the word *sepia*. But none of this is as remarkable or as jarring to the modern eye as the hump that issues from the base of his neck.

At once grotesque and perfectly formed, it's a hump that belongs more to fairy tales or Nazi physiognomy than it does to a living room in suburban Middlesex. As a kid I was obsessed with it. Every Friday dinner or Saturday breakfast I ate at my grandparents', there it was, looming over me, drawing my eye; a feature so big it had its own gravitational force. It filled me with a fear and disgust that Shakespeare would've approved of. I didn't play the piano but I made sure always to give it a passing stare – the same way I always made sure to lick square batteries and bite my fingers till they bled on my homework.

It was only a few years ago that I asked my grandpa about it. I did so casually, over Friday-night dinner, like the hump was just one detail I'd noticed about my great-grandfather. My grandpa Nat frowned like a garage door. What the hell was I talking about? His father wasn't a hunchback. Okay, well maybe not a *hunch*back – perhaps that was the wrong term – but then what would you call it? This time my brother backed me up – what *would* you call it? But my grandpa's frown only deepened. He looked afraid, like he thought either he or I might be having a stroke. Eventually my brother fetched the photo down from its perch on the piano to prove what really shouldn't have needed proving – and only then did we see it. The hump that for my whole life had been my great-grandfather's distinguishing feature wasn't a hump. It jutted from his shoulder like a limb because it *was* a limb. At the table behind him, dressed in an identical shade of charcoal, a man had his elbow cocked in such a way that it blended uncannily, although not-quite-seamlessly, into my zeyde's neck, creating the illusion that for twenty-odd years my brother and I had laboured under.

The odd part – although I suppose it's not so odd – was that even after I'd seen the thin border where my great-grandpa ended and the other man began, I couldn't think of him without thinking of the hump. Without his hump he was a stranger. Of course, he was a stranger already – he died before I was born and I knew nothing about him – but even after it was pointed out to me I couldn't stop seeing the hump. A few months ago, on my grandpa Nat's ninety-third birthday, I was watching my grandparents watch my son as he hammered away at the sharps and flats from his perch on Imogen's lap when my eyes drifted upwards to the frame that still sits on the piano's lid. 'That's your great-great-grandfather,' I told my son. 'The hunchback,' my brain supplied without hesitation.

It's not unusual to know nothing about your great-grandparents but it's even less unusual for European Jews to know nothing about their great-grandparents. We might read our prayer books from right to left like platform-game protagonists trying to revisit previous screens, but when it comes to family history there's only so far back most Jews can or dare go; you tend not to see a lot of European Jews on *Who Do You Think You Are?* since the story always ends the same way. I've come to think of the Holocaust as history's loudest full stop. But that's not to say I know nothing.

My family, I knew before writing this, hail from Poland, Russia and Czechoslovakia. Everyone I've never asked about – all those who didn't get out – met similar fates but unusually for a British Jew of my age all four of my grandparents were born in the UK. More unusually still, both of my great-grandfathers on my father's side fought for Britain in the First World War – we've even got letters one of them sent home to his wife. But my dad's parents are dead, and it isn't his zeyde who stared down at me my whole childhood, whom my son Arthur now sees whenever he visits his great-grandparents. Whom on recent trips he's started to ask about. I still don't know much about my zeyde but here's what I've learned.

He was born in Lublin, a small city in Poland, sometime in the 1890s. He spoke Hebrew and Yiddish. He trained as a tailor's apprentice. Tailoring involved working all hours. Often he would sleep under his workbench to ensure he was ready to start again when he woke up. He developed an interest in fashion and grew into a very presentable, dandyish young man. He had a walking stick he liked to use when he strolled around town (I always picture Patrick Macnee in *The Avengers*, although that might have been an umbrella). Sometime in the 1900s, in his late teens, he visited London with friends and there met an old acquaintance of his parents, a possible relative, who he came to know as his *feter* (uncle). After one look at Zeyde, his feter decided he'd make a good catch for a girl he knew back in Lublin. A marriage was arranged.

Beatings and killings of Jewish Poles were common, so too the plundering of Jewish households and businesses, sometimes by soldiers, sometimes civilians, and not long after he and Bubba married, these pogroms – a permanent feature of his childhood – intensified and Zeyde left Poland. At first he tried France but didn't like the morals so decided on London and sent for his wife to join him. On the journey over here, my bubba, who'd grown up in a *shtetl* (a small village with a nearly exclusive Jewish population), removed her *sheitel* (a wig some married Orthodox Jewish women wear to cover their hair) and cast it overboard as the boat hit the open sea. This, as I've always seen it, was her goodbye to the life she'd known, a casting off of the old world in preparation for the opportunities the new one promised.

In London they settled in the East End, in a flat in the curiously named Cannon Street Road. They found themselves in the middle of a newly established community of migrant Jews who'd come to Britain fleeing pogroms from across Central and Eastern Europe. There was a ghetto atmosphere to this part of the East End. Everyone was Jewish. The language on the streets was Yiddish. Zeyde found work in a tailoring business just off Brick Lane that years later became Simpsons of Piccadilly. He worked in a factory next to the bell house, which made and exported the Liberty Bell. They were poor, far poorer than they'd been in Poland, where at least they could eat, but there were no beatings and little fear of them; what anti-Semitism there was they were insulated from.

After the birth of their first son, Aaron, my great-uncle, Bubba and Zeyde moved to a flat in a terraced house in Chicksand Street. There were three floors of housing then workshops, the motto for which, mounted on the building's facade, was *Work Wait Win*, something my grandpa reflects on often: 'I know it's not the same but it has an echo, don't you think, of *Arbeit Macht Frei*.'

It was in this flat that my grandpa Nat and his four other siblings were born. Their parents gave each of them biblical names but they wouldn't stick. Aaron would be known as Harry, Israel became my great-uncle Jack and my grandpa Nat was born as Nissun. Now Bubba and Zeyde were poorer still but the children were blessed with good constitutions. To make ends meet, Bubba, a talented dressmaker, took on work as a seamstress, work she could do while at home with the kids, while Zeyde, when he wasn't at work, turned his affectation into a tool. In the area they lived some of the shops had basements that you could peer down into through a grate in the street. If he stuck a wad of gum to the handle of his cane, he discovered, he could fish for coins and anything else he might find that wasn't nailed down.

Like all immigrants, they wanted more for their children: although sometimes they couldn't eat, they found money for Harry to learn violin. It was important to expand their window on the world, not just to survive but to live. But it wasn't culture they'd come to England seeking, it was professions for their children that would offer security.[7] The garment trade was seasonal, and out of season there were no guarantees, so they wanted something that

---

7 I cringe to think that their great-grandson is a freelance writer.

provided their children more protections. Specifically, they wanted their sons, of which there were four, to enter the Civil Service. This would mean they would need to become British citizens. So in 1930, twenty years after bidding farewell to their homelands, they applied for their naturalisation papers, studied for their tests and became citizens, changing the family name from Senor to Singer.

Meanwhile, in religious terms, they lived a watered-down version of life in the shtetl. Every Saturday they paid a Shabbas goy to stoke the fire[8] and took their *cholent* (a traditional stew) to the bakers on Friday evening to cook in the ovens that were left cooling over the Sabbath. They also found money to send their sons to cheder several times a week, where they would half-heartedly learn Hebrew, occasionally stirred by the untrained teachers who incentivised with chocolate. As well as this they were sending money home to their families in Poland, those whose names I don't know.

It wasn't until my grandpa went to primary school that he first encountered non-Jews. This came as something of a shock: having been brought up speaking Yiddish, rarely venturing more than a hundred yards from his front door in an area that seemed exclusively Jewish, he didn't know he was different. He didn't advertise the fact he was Jewish but with his sharp features and thick, curly black hair he didn't look much like his classmates, who never treated him with malice or disgust – 'Although what their parents thought we never knew.' The Yiddish was a giveaway too. When

---

8   Religious Jews are forbidden from doing any physical work on the Sabbath and forbidden also from asking others to do it for them. (If you want a window opened you can try wiping your brow or fanning your shirt as a hint but you can't simply *ask* someone to open it.) Shabbas goys were usually children who would go from household to household performing small duties that had been previously agreed, earning a wage from each one. These were the first non-Jews my grandpa Nat ever knew.

an older boy stole from him, Nat (no longer Nissun) accused him of being a *ganev* (thief).

By the time of his bar mitzvah Nat's English had far out-stripped his parents'. He knew education was key to any success he might have and he understood his parents' obsession with him entering the Civil Service, even if he didn't quite know what the Civil Service was, so he applied himself to his studies. He excelled naturally in maths and science but read too and worked on his writing – though even with chocolate he gave up the Hebrew since it faced towards the past rather than the future. None of this is to say that he wasn't a *lobbus* (rascal). This side came out when he started washing in the public baths. For the first ten years of his life he lined up with his siblings by the kitchen sink every Friday for the weekly wash, but now he could wash in private in the luxury of a cubicle. Someone would walk up and down with a pail of hot water, topping up the baths of whoever needed it, and Nat would mangle his voice and call for hot water for a stranger's cubicle then sit back and wait for the screams.

He'd been born after the First World War had ended, but with the grim inevitability of a comic book franchise, the next instal-ment was on the way and promised a higher budget and greater destruction. Nat was thirteen in 1939, a man in the eyes of his com-munity, if not in those of his parents' adopted country. By 1940 the Admiralty were looking for youngsters who could be trained as the next generation of officers, and Nat's school put his name forward. This was to be his first time venturing beyond the walls of the ghetto that had raised him, and the experience was stark.

He was sent first to the Admiralty itself then to a training college in South London where he was taught physics, advanced mathematics and engineering. Again he excelled in his studies, but this wasn't what made him stand out. From growing up in an area where Yiddish was the primary language, he was the only Jew in a non-Jewish world, and he was soon made aware of his difference. His curly black locks made him popular with the girls but they undid what disguise the change of names had accomplished. At the Admiralty he was assigned originally to code-making and breaking but one look at him and the head of department reassigned him to something with a lower clearance where the work was mainly administrative. As Nat puts it, 'He took one look at me and he must've thought, "Fucking Jew, I don't want him on my team."'

But it was at the training centre in South London that tensions really escalated. At the Admiralty, Nat had been working alongside other working-class kids, but here were the higher classes, more educated and cosmopolitan. He expected better and got worse. At the Admiralty they'd sneered and made fun of him, called him a Jew like they were accusing him of a crime, but now he would be forced to fight. One day he came into class to find a question chalked on the board. Lord Moyne, the leader of the House of Lords, Secretary of State for the Colonies, had been assassinated by members of a Zionist paramilitary group best known as the Stern Gang, who wanted Britain out of Palestine and saw their presence there as an obstacle to Jewish immigration. It was something Nat was only dimly aware of. *Who killed Lord Moyne?* the board demanded. And underneath: *I say Nat*. He was jostled to the front of the class, handed gloves and made to box a succession of his classmates.

Much of Britain's self-image as a defender of liberalism and bastion of multiculturalism comes from winning the Second World War; because we defeated the Nazis, we're the good guys. In fact, Britain has never really recovered from this. We're encouraged to think of ourselves as tolerant and welcoming while living in a country where the bestselling newspapers routinely compare migrants to floods and swarms, and governments left and right are lambasted for failing to deliver on their targets for restricting immigration. Even in 2014's *Paddington*, that adorable, sweetshop-coloured ode to British neighbourliness and open-heartedness, émigré Paddington isn't truly accepted by his community until he's proven his good citizenry by apprehending a pickpocket, played by Super Hans from *Peep Show*.

And so it proved for Nat. 'These were the so-called better classes, the people who were supposed to be more tolerant. I can still remember the look on one of their faces. He was so anti-Semitic it was written right across him.' This was the day he started to question his commitment to the country of his birth, the only home he'd ever known, and his willingness to fight, possibly give his life, for a cause that saw him as less than equal. He was vaguely aware what was happening on the continent, in the lands of his grandparents, but to mistake Britain as a bastion of acceptance was a mistake he could no longer make in good conscience.

He managed to arrange for his end-of-course physical to be taken in King's Cross, away from his classmates. To enter on to the course he'd had to pass a physical and some exams; he'd performed so well in these that he'd been suspected of cheating. But in this final assessment before he could graduate into the army, following a performance that must have rivalled his one decades later in a cinema in Garston, he was graded 3 – *psychologically unfit for military service*. How did he convince them? 'It was common knowledge that Jews were neurotic. It was common knowledge at the time that, psychologically, Jews were quite highly strung . . .'

As it happened, the war was nearly over and Nat spent the next few months doing what work he could get to keep a roof over his head. There was a stigma attached to shirkers and no one would hire him. His sister Doris had a friend who had some handbags to sell and he set himself to making a success of it. He stood in shop doorways, demeaning himself, hardening himself, realising he'd do anything to make something of his circumstance, but it came to nothing. He got hold of some cough sweets, bought some scales, and set up shop in Roman Street Market.

His older brother Harry, who'd developed a lifelong stutter after his interrogation by two policemen following an accusation of dishonest dealings made by a neighbour, had been graded 3 also and was working for a dressmaker in the East End. Every week Harry travelled across London, to the West End, the epicentre of ladies' fashion, where he'd collect the rolls of cloth needed to fill orders for a certain number of dresses. Through skilful cutting he was able to make *cabbage* – the material for one or two extra – so Nat taught himself to cut and sew. Again he was a quick learner and soon, with his sister Doris, he'd formed Nador Gowns. He'd hawk their handiwork all over London, facing the humiliation of taking crowded Tubes with his arms full of samples while his competitors were in cars and taxis. But the work was good and they earned a contract from a West End house that was looking to outsource.

It was a family venture: my great-uncle Jack, who'd served in the air force as an accountant, set them up with a workshop; their brother Ben's wife cut the first pattern; a family friend fitted them out with machines; and Bubba lent her expert eye to finishing and buttons. More orders followed, which meant more hands on deck, and before long Nat was putting his officer training to good use by running a factory.

It was also in the Admiralty that Nat had decided he'd never work in the Civil Service; instead he would go into business. If he couldn't control what people thought of him he could at least control how they acted around him. 'If I run a business and people want what I'm selling they'll have to behave.' Jack, through a benefactor in the ghetto, had landed a job in the City after the air force, but was bullied there and lost the position after punching a superior, and decided that he too wanted to be in business for himself. He got a job in a clothes factory with the idea of learning how it was run and he soon worked his way up the ranks. But this was the *shmutter* business, the same capricious beast his parents had become naturalised in order that their children might escape; he needed something less seasonal.

So Jack opened a shoe shop in Blackstock Road, Finsbury Park. Ben, who would later kill himself, had failed the Civil Service exam but was a skilled salesman. Business was steady and, seeing what his brothers were doing, Nat wanted to learn. He helped out on Saturdays (he was long past the point of relying on Shabbas goys) and when the boys opened a second branch in Stoke Newington he came on full-time.

Most of my favourite stories that my grandpa tells come from his time running the shop in Stoke Newington, but like his feelings towards Britain and his service in the war, I'm nervous about sharing them. Not for any legal reasons – I'm sure there's a statute of limitations on the misdemeanours I'm about to describe – but for fear of who might be listening. Minorities always need to be aware of those who extrapolate from an individual's actions in order to reinforce their negative feelings towards a group. This means that all minorities must be mindful of the stories we tell, and of their potential audience, which is something non-minorities, who operate inside far wider spectrums of expected behaviour, need never consider. But it's important to remember that Jews are Jews second and people first – and important too, I think, to tell the story as accurately as I can.

Nat was never what you might call honest to a fault. Like Howard Ratner, the protagonist of the Safdie brothers' 2019 masterwork *Uncut Gems* (a timely study of the ways minorities internalise trauma and, occasionally, turn it to their advantage), he did what he could to win. This was a time before trading standards and Nat took full advantage. He soon realised that it didn't pay to keep a full range of sizes stocked when, pre-internet, you knew

35

more than the customer could ever hope to. A full range then was a Three, a Five and a Seven; if you had the misfortune to wander into his shop, you were leaving with one of them – if the Five was too small then you fetched the next size up: the Seven. If that was too big you went back to the Five. (There was no leaving without making a purchase.) In summer, if a customer's feet didn't fit into the smaller shoe you needed to sell, you got them to rest their feet in a bucket of cold water.[9]

Their biggest sellers were Hush Puppies but since everyone sold Hush Puppies, even butchers and bakers, there was barely a margin, so Nat sent his manufacturer a pattern and ordered a hundred pairs of Brush Piggies. The Hush Puppy and the Brush Piggy sat beside each other in the window and when you came in for a dog he sold you a hog.[10]

This continued until the Cease and Desist letter but it didn't stop him for long. He pulled a similar stunt with two other brands called Tuf and Gluv, deflecting customers from the cheaper with the smaller margins to the dearer with the larger, and sometimes selling them the cheaper regardless of what they'd paid. At first the shoe shop was another family operation but soon they were taking on staff, but, as he told me – deadpan like all the best jokes – 'I never asked anyone to do anything I wouldn't be comfortable doing myself.'

In the interests of balance, my other grandfather, sadly no longer with us, made Immanuel Kant look like P.T. Barnum. He served in the Admiralty from 1945 and received an exemplary discharge,

---

9   In Kilburn, where they later opened a branch, the largely Irish clientele would try the shoes on by putting their hands inside them, but they never thought to repeat the trick.

10 I sometimes wonder, or I'm starting to wonder, if the Brush Piggy was the sublimation of some latent guilt about letting go of his religion. They were called Piggies and they weren't kosher.

marred only by criticism from an officer he'd caught and bowled in an intramural cricket match. He told me one time, unusually lucid on painkillers after an operation on his prostate, that he'd once had the chance to take a large sum of money, with no possibility that it could be traced back to him, from his job of twenty years' standing. The story, ostensibly, was about the importance of staying honest but it sounded to me, at least in part, like a regret.

That's not to say I think of my grandpa Nat as crooked or that I'm in any way ashamed of his dealings, or that I have anything but sympathy (and gratitude) for the choices he's made, partially by circumstance and partially by character. His worldview was informed by the fact he was made to feel unwelcome in the only home he'd ever known and I can understand if this instilled a sense of pre-emptive contempt. He saw himself as at odds with a society that frequently treated him with suspicion and derision. And besides, now he had a family to provide for.

In 1954, he'd met a girl at a dance in Hendon. Helen was born in Bethnal Green in 1935 to my great-grandma Golda – the only great-grandparent I remember, albeit vaguely (a child's-eye view à la *Tom and Jerry*, Sunday visits and smuggled sweets)[11] – and my great-grandpa Davis. Both Golda and Davis had been born in the UK and raised in the East End: Golda by Lithuanian émigrés who'd moved to Britain in the 1890s, again fleeing pogroms; and Grandpa Davis (which is how my grandma refers to him) by Austrian Jews of the same era. Both were raised religious and in poverty in the same ghetto that Bubba and Zeyde were transplanted into, and when they didn't want my grandma or her siblings to know what they were saying they reverted to Yiddish, their parents' only tongue. Golda learned English in school and was training to be a teacher

---

11 She lived in Golders Green and I used to think the *s* was possessive: *Golda's Green*.

but dropped out to take a job as a machinist in a fur factory ('more like two rooms above a shop'), which was run by a former chamber-master, Herman Wasserman – my great-great-grandfather. There she fell in love with the boss's son.

They got married and moved to a house in Upper Clapton and were quite well-off until 1934, when Grandpa Davis went to collect a debt from his largest client and was chased off the premises with a gun. He was forced into insolvency, his business folded and they moved back to a small terrace in Bethnal Green, where Helen, my mum's mum, was born the following year, and raised with her two brothers and her sister Kaye, who was really her cousin. This wasn't quite like the ghetto – their upstairs neighbours weren't Jewish, and while she played with their sons in the street, Helen was forbidden from entering their home. But as far as my grandma knew, hers was a typically strict religious upbringing. On Fridays they lit candles, Grandma Golda kept separate sets of cutlery and crockery for meat and milk, and at Passover time the house was in turmoil: the bath was off-limits for three days and nights as she soaked the glassware in preparation for the Seder.

When Helen was four, her father was called up and she was evacuated, first to County Durham then to the suburbs of Manchester. She wasn't aware of being treated any differently because she was Jewish, nor was she when she returned to London after the war, to Ealing, though again she played in the streets with the neighbourhood children but was never invited into their homes, nor did they come back to hers. When she was ten (and Nat was twenty), the Stern Gang hanged two soldiers, and a close friend knocked at the door and told her from the street that they could no longer be friends. Helen didn't understand why; if Davis and Golda had ever discussed what had happened during the war they'd done so in Yiddish and all Helen knew was from the newsreel footage that played before the feature in the cinema in Ealing. (Children were sent out of the cinema but Helen, always curious, had peeked back through a crack in the door.)

She was the only Jewish girl at her primary school and one of only two at the grammar she was accepted to after her eleven-plus – they gravitated towards each other but the other girl was later expelled – and it was in Ealing that she first started seeking the company of other Jewish youngsters. She went to cheder, ostensibly to learn Hebrew, and started attending Jewish clubs and youth groups around North London (all named for Israel, which was about to achieve statehood). 'I knew on some level, subconsciously, I was supposed to be around Jews.'

Her uncle Jack had fought in the First World War and had met a non-Jewish girl who he later married. Her parents didn't sit *shiva* (a period of mourning that follows a Jewish funeral) as some families might've, but there was no more word either of him or from him – to all intents she no longer had an uncle. Similarly, her cousin Kaye, raised as her sister, had been abandoned by Helen's aunt Ray, who'd moved to Ireland before the war and severed ties with her first family – partly, Helen suspects, because 'she didn't want her new family finding out she was Jewish'.

At sixteen Helen got a job in the Registry at NATO as an international Civil Servant (a job Bubba and Zeyde would have dreamed of for Nat), but when the Registry moved to Belgium, and with her mother ill, she found a new job through an agency that specialised in finding posts that allowed for Sabbath observance working for a German–Jewish refugee: the lavishly named Wolfgang Herman Kugelman. Before the war, Wolfgang had run a department store in Bonn but he'd lost everything to the Nazis and he now imported Jean Patou perfumes and Hermès scarves. And this was where she was working, probably with Jean Patou on her wrists, when she attended a dance at the Brent Bridge Hotel in Hendon . . .

'I was attracted to her straightaway,' says Nat, who'd almost certainly snuck into the dance through a side door, 'because she was tearing up napkins.'

And what did Helen make of the black-haired older man who strode over and asked her to dance and later invited her on a date to the cinema to see *Anna and the King of Siam*, on Yom Kippur, the holiest day of the Jewish calendar? 'Well, he looked nice enough. A bit old maybe. I remember when I brought him home that's what Grandpa Davis told me. I told him not to worry, "I'm only going out with him, I'm not going to marry him."'

They were married two years later, back at the Brent Bridge Hotel. Four years after that my mum, Joanne, was born, and eighteen years after that Joanne met my dad, Mike, at a party his girlfriend was throwing, in the girlfriend's bedroom while she (the girlfriend) was asleep in the bed – but that's another story for another book. Nat didn't care if they kept a kosher household and Helen didn't care where they lived so long as their children could 'find Jewish friends without having to look'. They settled on Canons Park and set about raising their kids as Jewish as they knew how, which was how Helen realised her upbringing wasn't as *frum* as she'd thought: she couldn't read Hebrew and had never said a prayer. Both she and Nat had lapsed from the ghetto attitude that, far more than the religion itself, had kept their families Jewish, but it was still important to them that both their children were raised Jewish with an understanding of what being Jewish meant to them.

They cut corners where they had to – they didn't have the money to buy two sets of plates so bought glass ones, which could be used for both meat and milk – and there was always an argument when Nat had to work on Rosh Hashanah and Yom Kippur, but when Bubba and Zeyde were too old to make Seders themselves, it was to my grandparents' house that they came.

Judaism was less a religion than a way of life, the only one Nat and Helen had ever known. It was like a glue or an interplanetary force, a form of gravity that held the family in orbit, stopped them all from spinning out into space. And it was forward-looking as much as retroactive: these days my grandparents keep kosher not for their parents or ancestors who died long ago but for my mum and my brother. As my grandma puts it, 'The family doesn't serve the religion, the religion serves the family.' It reminds me of one my favourite jokes: a religious man – let's call him Wolfgang Kugelman – attends synagogue every week but has a penchant for the honey-glazed pork at the restaurant next door. One day he's sitting down to eat when his rabbi walks past the window . . . just as the waiter is delivering the works: the whole beast, with an apple in its mouth, on a bed of lettuce and resting on a silver platter. 'Rabbi,' says Kugelman, 'have you ever seen an apple served so beautifully?'

So what would they have thought if my mum or my uncle had married out?

First, my grandpa: 'It would've upset us. It didn't matter so much with your mother because her children would've been Jewish anyway [Jewishness is matrilineal so if your mum's Jewish, so are you] but still, it would've upset us. Plenty of people, if they got an invitation for a mixed marriage, they'd throw it in the bin . . . They wouldn't even look at it. I don't think we'd have done that . . .'

So what would they have done if my uncle Neil had come home with a non-Jewish girl and announced their engagement?

My grandma Helen, who rarely minces her words and whose voice I approximate for Mother Hen every time I read *Chocolate Mousse for Greedy Goose* to Arthur: 'I'd probably have tried to talk him out of it.' A pause. 'And if he'd insisted . . .' Another pause, during which I realise I'm holding my breath. 'I'd have accepted it. Because he's my son. It's like you and Imogen. I'd have preferred it if you had found someone Jewish – it would have been nice. I can remember hearing so many times as a youngster: a man marries out and the new family say you're fantastic, wonderful, my best friend's a Jew; but have a stand-up, face-to-face argument with them and they'll call you a bloody Jew . . . I love Imogen and you're very happy and that is the main thing. In this day and age you accept things that you wouldn't have thirty, forty years ago. It's a way of life. Society's changed. We've become more tolerant. Nothing is forever.'

My grandpa again, who's rarely the one to interrupt: 'I realise now that happiness is the prime thing. The religion is important. But happiness is more important . . . Look, it's not the end of the world.'

Chapter Three:
Comedy

When I was nineteen I wrote a play with my best friend called *Other People*. You won't have heard of it but it changed the course of our lives. *Other People* was a comic two-hander about two twenty-something flatmates (how old they seemed to us!): one with a respectable job, some savings and a fiancée; the other alone and underemployed as a bad live statue – the joke, which we were inordinately proud of, was that he was standing still in every aspect of his life except for in his job, where he couldn't stop fidgeting and was always getting into fights.

The characters weren't Jewish – it never occurred to us that they should be – but both my friend and I were and so too, it seems hard to ignore, was a certain sensibility. The humour, for two nineteen-year-olds, was world-weary and self-lacerating: Michael, the live statue, who we gave all the best lines, was a paranoid outsider railing against the world from a position of material comfort within it. He'd been replaced in his job as a lollypop man by a pelican crossing; conga lines ground to a halt at the moment he joined them. At nineteen we were bemoaning the end of our youths; it was a wrench for both characters that they were no longer eligible to be selected for the England U21 squad.

After performing the play to modest laughs at our respective universities, we decided to invite financial ruin by taking it to the Edinburgh Fringe Festival, where we performed it to twenty people a day in a converted hotel conference suite and where, by some kismet that at the time looked like good fortune but in retrospect may not have been, it garnered reasonable reviews; two of the reviewers compared it to *Men Behaving Badly* and on the train back to Hertfordshire on the last day of the festival we received a call from a man claiming to be its producer. Did we have any London dates? he wanted to know. Of course, we lied, and promptly set about pleading with a local arts centre, just within the M25, to let us stage it one last time.

Through this unlikely turn of events we gained representation and an option deal with Talkback Thames to turn our modest two-hander into a world-conquering sitcom. But the next year, down on our luck again, the option having come to nothing, we decided to return to what we already thought of as our roots.

Other People never touched on theology or religious identity – the closest it came was in a throwaway line from a disgruntled RE teacher: 'Jesus died for your mum' – but the next year, in a sequel of sorts, we circled closer. This time the action was set either side of a heroes-and-villains-themed fancy-dress party. The first act was mostly dedicated to a discussion of what the characters would wear. Jonathan, the better adjusted of the pair, would attend as his child-hood hero, Indiana Jones, while Michael, the *nebbish*, couldn't decide. Eventually he settled on Adolf Eichmann, mostly because he was the architect of the Holocaust, but partly also because the character felt some strange, sympathetic affinity towards him: he was the lesser Adolf.

The action of the play's second half began with Michael in a ripped SS uniform and sporting a matured black eye, as he removed his swastika and threw it despondently to the floor. This always got a big laugh, as did Jonathan's entrance, still in character as Indiana Jones ('Nazis, I hate these guys!'). But the biggest laugh was always reserved for the eventual reveal. The party had taken place in the function room of a large hotel, outside which, smoking, sleeve concealed, Michael had got talking to a waiter. One thing had led to another and his jacket was removed, revealing his armband, which precipitated a hasty retreat from the suddenly no longer amorous waiter. Michael had followed, into the wrong room where another function was in full swing. At this point Jonathan picked up the story:

> JONATHAN (through his hands): Kids' party? Wedding? Wake?

> MICHAEL (pause, almost triumphant): Bar mitzvah.

This time the reviews were better and attendances stronger, so the next year we wrote another one. Our ambitions growing out of proportion with our talent, we hired a larger space and enlisted a cast and another co-writer for a feature-length farce based on an idea my friend had talked about for a while. We both knew families, not dissimilar to ours, in which assimilation was considered a bigger threat than extermination; who believed that 'marrying out' was letting Hitler win. What if, within one of these families, the only son was engaged to a non-Jewish woman (a *shiksa*, as they would have it), and what if, rather than bite the bullet and introduce her to his parents, he came out as gay?

The idea was not that Jews were homophobic (they are or aren't to the same extent as everyone else; culturally, it's less about sexuality than creation, less *homo-* versus *hetero-* than *pro-* versus *re-*), but that the thought of not having grandchildren would upset our hero's parents to such an extent that when he revealed the truth they'd be so relieved they'd welcome his fiancée with open arms – since Jews, as all Jews know, are under greater pressure to breed than pandas in captivity.

Of course, this being a farce, the plan backfires: firstly, on hearing the news, his mum dies of a heart attack. Secondly, at her shiva, inspired by his son's courage, the father comes out of the closet. Unable to reveal that he's killed his mother in a hoax, the son, Simon, a paediatrician (itself a great disappointment to his parents: 'He couldn't be a real doctor?'), continues with the sham engagement to his roommate (who, in true farce tradition, is secretly in love with him), culminating in a wedding, which is only averted when, for reasons too convoluted to explain, it's revealed that Simon's mother, she of the dicky heart and rampant anti-goyism, was adopted at birth and therefore, technically, was not Jewish herself. At this point an epiphany dawns. Jewishness, like baldness or cystic fibrosis, is passed down the mother's line and if Simon's mother wasn't Jewish then neither, technically, is he. His father protests: 'You are . . . It doesn't matter . . . It's who you are . . . It's how we raised you.' But Simon can't hear him. Like a flashback montage at the end of an M. Night Shyamalan film, his whole Jewish life is replaying before him:

> *My bar mitzvah . . . Sunday mornings at cheder . . . Not eating pork . . . (building to an epiphany) GIVE ME BACK MY FORESKIN!*

That line was workshopped in rehearsal but the rest of the play's ninety minutes, as with the two previous plays and countless drafts of our disastrous sitcom, we'd written surrounded by listing towers of file boxes in the attic of my friend's dad's accountancy firm. At first this was a matter of convenience – we both still lived at home, surrounded by our childhood film collections and games consoles – but pretty soon it became part of our praxis. The office had a reception area that faced the street, beyond which my friend's dad did sums and saw clients. There was a window-less middle office sometimes occupied by an intern, two toilets, a communal kitchenette where we met to make tea or heat up our lunches, and a back office that, via a fire door, gave on to an always empty alleyway. Out of this back office my friend's grandpa ran a stationery business. Between scenes or after a par-ticularly gruelling hour arguing over whether *wiener* or *johnson* made for a superior punchline, we'd boil water for his sachets of soups and help him load his blue van, which was parked at the alleyway's end. Once or twice we accompanied him on deliveries. I remember collecting his van from somewhere once but I can't remember where or why.

My friend's grandpa was (*is*) called Zigi and is among the friendliest people I know. When I think of him I think of a phrase I've only ever heard used in a negative context, but applied here is wholly positive: I spent a month with him one afternoon. My friend Darren, the same one who barters with God over football scores, likes to joke that everyone who's ever shared a train carriage with Zigi knows the story of his life and the subjects his grand-children (and now his great-grandchildren) are enjoying in school. By the time we worked there he was well past retirement age, late seventies, early eighties, but couldn't conceive of stopping and no one dared suggest it. Working got him out of the house and into the world. As far as I could tell he had a few loyal clients, who no longer needed him but doubtless enjoyed the gregariousness he

47

brought to his deliveries. Maybe it was his rhotic Rs which you could see gathering like breakers, or his idiosyncratic English that still revealed itself in certain constructions ('Or we're eating dinner or we're watching the game!'),[12] but there was something about him that made you feel at once incongruous and accepted, like you were the one living outside of time.

As I say, Zigi would never have dreamed of retiring but his real job, the one he didn't get paid for, involved travelling the country to speak to schoolchildren about his childhood. Born in Lodz, Poland, in 1930, Zigi had lived with his father and grandparents in an apartment with a yard where he used to play with other children. His life, as he remembers it, was comfortable, until the age of nine when he woke to find his father standing at the foot of his bed wearing his coat and hat. He had to go, he told his son. The Germans were coming and would kill him if they found him. Like many, Zigi's father believed that the Germans wouldn't harm the women and children. He made it to Russia and later attempted to get back to Lodz to be with his son but got only as far as Warsaw, which was the last Zigi heard of him.

School had closed over the summer and never reopened and it was soon obvious that Zigi's life had changed for good. With his grandparents he was ordered to leave the apartment he'd been born in and move to a designated area of the city called Baluty, which became known as the Lodz Ghetto. You know how the story goes but it's important to listen. His grandfather died not long after from lack of nutrition, around which time, at the age of ten, Zigi started a job in the Ghetto's metal factory, working towards the German war effort. Lorryloads of Jews arrived at the Ghetto from neighbouring towns but to deal with the

---

12 It reminded me of the phrases I remembered from my great-grandma Golda: *in the furnace of time*; *no point making a solemn dance.*

overcrowding, which, along with the malnutrition, led to high rates of death and disease, the Germans started sending Jews for 'resettlement'.

One week in 1941, during one of these resettlement drives, Zigi was taken from his home (the one room he shared with his grandma and several other families) and loaded on to the back of a truck. 'I don't know what made me do it but I managed to jump off.' He ran several miles and hid. Eventually he returned to the metal factory, where he remained until 1944 when, with the Russians approaching, the Nazis decided to liquidate the Ghetto. Along with his grandmother and his fellow factory workers, Zigi was herded to the train station where the cattle trucks awaited. This time there was no escape.

Days later, Zigi arrived at Auschwitz-Birkenau to be greeted by the sight of distant chimneys billowing smoke. Viktor Frankl in *Man's Search For Meaning* talks about camps with chimneys and camps without but at fourteen Zigi's first thought was that someone was baking fresh bread. He was made to line up for selection, separated from his grandmother, who he never saw again, and told to undress. He was shaved, disinfected and sent to be showered. Again he was lucky: the 'shower' really was a shower. He was given his striped pyjamas, told to learn the number sewn to them (84303), and assigned a bunk, which he shared with eight other inmates.

A few weeks later he was loaded back on to a cattle truck and transferred to another camp called Stutthof, where conditions were even worse. It was November 1944 and so bitterly cold that the only way to survive outside, where Zigi spent all day waiting for instruction, was by making human kilns: several dozen inmates would huddle together, each taking their turn to stand in the middle. His prospects were so bleak that when Nazi officers came looking for child workers for a new labour camp, he volunteered. He was transferred again, this time by train, to a railway yard in a place called Stolp. At least here he had work to keep him warm and the opportunity to steal some food (until now he'd survived, just barely, on a slice of bread morning and evening), but some of the horrors he witness here would haunt him for the rest of his life; like the time the camp was assembled to watch the hanging of five boys who'd been caught stealing cigarettes from a train bound for the front.

In March 1945 he was returned to Stutthof, where conditions had deteriorated: now, as well as no food, there was no water, and Russian bombs were falling day and night. A month later he was taken, in the back of a lorry, to another camp called Burschgrabben. This one was so close to the Russian front that at night they could hear music. From there he was transferred to Danzig then, on foot, to Gdynia, where he was put on a barge and sent out to sea. By this point most of his cohort, Zigi included, had typhus and after ten days at sea with no food or water, and, as ever, with no idea where they were going, many drank sea water and became sicker still. By night the German officers would leave the barges by boat to go back to land, and one night, aided by the far healthier Danish and Norwegian prisoners of war who were on the barge too, Zigi and some others made it ashore. When the Germans found them there the next morning they ordered another march to a town fifteen kilometres away. Had Zigi fallen on this march he would've been shot, and again it was his great good fortune that he had friends who would drag him along on their shoulders.

Eventually he made it to a naval town called Neustadt, which was now being bombed by the British. 'One bomb hit the boat that we were supposed to go on, which already had people from other camps on it . . . People were jumping off the boat to try to get to shore. We were looking up at what was happening and people were shouting and yelling, it seemed with joy – they were waving things.' He turned round and could no longer see Nazis, just British tanks. It was 3 May 1945 and he was about to be liberated.

There were still many deaths to come. In the days after liberation many died from eating too fast – after so much suffering it was freedom that was fatal – but that night Zigi slept in his own bunk, in clean white sheets; he woke the next morning to find them black and crawling with lice. In the prison in which he was housed (though this time not as a prisoner), he was treated for his typhus and regained strength enough to be transferred again to a children's home near Neustadt with forty other Jewish survivors.

It was here that he received a letter with an English postmark from a woman claiming to be his mother, who'd left him when he was five. She couldn't be certain but she remembered an incident with a stove. If he had a burn mark on his left wrist then it was likely he was her son. He checked his wrist and found the mark. He'd already decided to go to Palestine, where all his friends were preparing to be sent, but they persuaded him to change his mind: he had a chance to have a mother. Watching them leave was the saddest moment of his life.

A few weeks later he boarded a boat to Hull, where he was met by his stepfather. 'The first thing I remember him asking was, "Where is your luggage?" I burst out laughing and replied in Yiddish, "What I'm wearing is what I have."'

◆ ◆ ◆

I'd known Zigi for more than a decade and worked in the office above him for several years before I first heard him tell this story. At an event organised by HET, the Holocaust Educational Trust, in front of an audience of schoolchildren and organisers, he shuffled onstage, this most gregarious of men who'd never complained of a moment's suffering in his life, suddenly old. The first time my parents had told me about the Holocaust, when I was maybe eight or nine, I distinctly remember I thought they were exaggerating. 'They didn't actually try to *kill* us,' I scoffed, appalled by the melodramatics. 'They *did*,' they insisted, 'and they succeeded.' 'But not in our *millions*?' This was the word people used in the playground to boast or exaggerate; I'd never heard it outside of that context. 'Yes, in our millions.' And now here was this man I thought I knew well who'd lived through the things I couldn't bring myself to imagine, and who considered himself the luckiest person alive.

Two things stayed with me most: the relief he admitted to feeling on that first cattle train to Auschwitz when other passengers died, because at least now, once the bodies were thrown on the tracks, there was somewhere to sit; and the way he described watching his friends being hanged in that railyard. How they each jumped from their stools to deny the Nazis the pleasure of their murder.

There's a theory of comedy that dates back to the playground that essentially has it as a defensive manoeuvre. An evolutionary tactic to deflect the bully's attention. It makes sense to think of Jewish humour in this way, only in our case the playground is history – or maybe history's the bully. It's not that all Jews are funny or that only Jews are funny, it's that there are modes of being funny that are recognisably Jewish. Sometimes this is a criticism. Studio notes on the pilot of *Seinfeld*, the sitcom about nothing that always tops polls of the greatest of all time and whose finale would be watched in more households than the moon landings (or any other of Kubrick's films), dismissed it as 'too New York, too Jewish'. But years before *Seinfeld*, Jewish comedians were honing and breaking the rules of modern comedy, first in the 'Borscht Belt', the faux-alpine resorts where Jewish immigrant families were allowed to holiday in the 1940s, '50s and '60s,[13] then in the cities to mixed audiences too.

Jewish comedy is diffuse and easier to spot than define but is usually characterised by a world-weariness, albeit worn lightly – less as resignation or depression than tacit approval. Drama requires desire but comedy can come from acceptance. It's anger turned upside down and inside out. And a lot of it is self-directed. Some of my favourite Jewish jokes (or 'jokes' as we call them) rely on negative stereotypes. Take the Jewish grandmother who directs her grandson to her new apartment via a series of elbow-related instructions: 'With your right elbow, you'll hail the taxi . . . With your left elbow you'll call the lift . . . With your right elbow you'll knock on the door . . .' 'What's with all the elbows?' the grandson asks eventually. 'What?' exclaims the grandma. 'You're coming empty-handed?' Some might see this as offensive, playing as it does with notions of greed, or at best unhelpful, but I prefer to think of it as jumping from the stool.

If great art comes from great suffering then for every Muddy Waters or Billie Holiday there's a Groucho Marx or Mel Brooks. 'These are my principles and if you don't like them I have others,' quipped Groucho, and while Alvy Singer chose another Marx line for his 'key joke' in the Oscar-winning *Annie Hall*, no other joke cuts quicker to the heart of comedy as survival. Comedy requires polysemy, being in two places at once, and so too does survival. In the early modern period, court Jews were afforded special privileges (read *protections*) for providing financial counsel to nobles

---

13 Restrictions meant their choices of where to stay were limited.

and monarchs. Their survival was contingent on occupying two simultaneous positions: at once the insider and the 'other', never sure when the worm might turn and their privileges (read *protections*) be revoked.

Comedy can be a tool for survival not just in the sense that it brings comfort and offers a reason to endure through suffering, but in the way it can allow you to co-exist with a difficult principle, to live between incompatible positions. In *Man's Search for Meaning*, Viktor Frankl, also an Auschwitz survivor, writes repeatedly of humour's place in the arsenal of tools any inmate needed to survive the camps: more than any other tool in the human arsenal, it 'can afford an aloofness and an ability to rise above any situation, even if only for a few seconds'.

He goes on to recall how he trained a friend who worked beside him on a brutal work detail to use humour to gain a vantage on his suffering by suggesting that each day they invent a funny story about something that might occur to them after they'd been liberated. His friend was a surgeon and to amuse him Frankl invited him to imagine how his present suffering might inform his future behaviour. One day, he told him, you might be performing a surgery and an orderly will rush into the theatre and announce the arrival of a more senior surgeon by shouting 'Action! Action!' – the words the foreman of their building site used to announce the arrival of a guard and encourage them to work faster. The ability to maintain a humorous outlook, Frankl writes, 'is a trick learned while mastering the art of living'.

And at the same time as consolation or a different vantage, comedy brings ownership. This can be true of self-deprecation and reclaiming negative stereotypes, but also of philosophical tenets: in owning the absurdity of a godless universe you can draw comfort from its lack of feeling, or at least from your acceptance of it. God and godlessness has long been a source of humour for Jewish comedians (in his genius *2000 Year Old Man* improvisations, Mel Brooks's former cave-dweller jokes about worshipping a man named Phil who one day is struck by lightning, prompting the realisation that 'there's something bigger than Phil'), but the subject perhaps receives its most sustained and thorough examination in the nihilistic slapstick of mid-career Woody Allen.[14]

The first Woody Allen film I saw was during my first week as a student at an empty screening in the on-campus arts centre, which the night before had seen queues up the street for the second part of *The Motorcycle Diaries*. I was invited by a new (non-Jewish) friend who'd assumed I was a fan of his work, possibly because she knew me better than I knew myself, or possibly because so many of the performers on whom I'd subconsciously based my persona had consciously based theirs on his. The film was *Anything Else*, the end of one of his early late-period revivals.[15] Its plot was a rehash of earlier, better films, it featured an awkward, inconsistent voiceover and at times seemed barely professional, but it spoke to me in a way that almost nothing I'd seen had, especially the final scene. The Woody Allen character, one of two, this one played by Jason Biggs fresh from making love to a pastry case in *American Pie* (released just four years earlier), glimpses his ex-wife and her new partner from the back of a passing taxi and starts to laugh. 'What's so funny?' the taxi driver

---

14 I'm not interested in discussing his possible crimes here or the deep problems with many fans' reactions to them but I would urge you to read Claire Dederer's brilliant essay in the November 2017 issue of *The Paris Review*, 'What Do We Do With the Art of Monstrous Men?'

15 If anyone tells you their favourite Woody Allen film is *Match Point* or *Midnight in Paris*, run.

wants to know. Biggs can't answer. 'Life,' he offers up. The taxi driver shrugs. 'Well, it's like anything else.'

This line alone was enough that I promptly sought out the classics: *Annie Hall*, *Radio Days*, *Hannah and Her Sisters* . . . They introduced me to ways of being funny and looking at the world I'd only seen in imitation, and in the Woody Allen characters I'd finally found a hero I could relate to; an on-screen avatar whose concerns were my own but that I'd failed to articulate. The anxiety, the kibitzing, the tics and hand jabs that suggested an overactive thyroid disorder: this was the Jewish identity I recognised, the tradition I wanted to belong to.

I devoured his films. I showed them to friends. I referenced them to potential partners and gauged their reactions. Before long, though, I started to notice something. It wasn't just that the films grew weaker as I worked my way down the IMDb rankings, though unquestionably they did, it was that my relationship with the Woody on-screen began to change. What at first I'd found so appealing – the tics and awkwardness, the pure, unfiltered, never-from-concentrate *nebbish* of it all – started to grate. From film to film it was a copy of itself, self-plagiarism, art imitating art, but that wasn't it exactly, or at least not entirely. More and more it felt like an articulation of someone else's idea.

In *Anything Else* there's a cathartic scene in which Biggs's mentor, played by Woody Allen himself, takes revenge on two neckless toughs who steal his parking spot by smashing their windscreen with a tyre iron, but this was the exception that proved the rule – the anti-Woody being played by Woody as a joke. The real Woody is Biggs, who suggests they write a biting satire that exposes their enemies' foibles, and lambasts his friend from the safety of the passenger seat. This was the Woody of *Annie Hall*, the ur-nebbish: physically weak, terrified of confrontation, seafood, even arachnids. ('There's a spider in your bath the size of a Buick!') In short, first and foremost, the nebbish was not a threat. But what initially had seemed like an encapsulation of everything I saw in myself, and a celebration of it, was something else: a performance. And who, I soon started to wonder, was this performance for?

The nebbish, as I understand it now, that staple of Jewish comedy, never better portrayed than Alvy in *Annie Hall*, has a darker underside. In the same way that camp is a performance of gayness that seems at first to celebrate identity but also limits its scope, the nebbish presents a culturally acceptable form of being Jewish whose primary audience is non-Jews. Like camp, it does several things at once: broadcasts its Jewishness without making it explicit; exaggerates expected traits, and demands that attention be paid it. But primarily it announces that the Jew is present. (There are no non-Jewish nebbishes, although Eddie Murphy does a decent impression in the underrated *Bowfinger*.) In this way it's like a klaxon, a reverse dog whistle, one blown by the dog to attract a leash.[16]

It dates from a time when Jews *needed* to signal that they weren't a threat, that they were comically weak and compliant.[17] How much of this did I internalise before I realised there was only one culturally sanctioned way of being Jewish? (Why did we have

---

16 There's an argument to be made, in fact, that anti-Semitism operates more like homophobia than traditional racism. In both cases the 'otherness' often isn't visual, meaning both groups usually have the choice of if and when to disclose it, which means both are often subject to discriminatory language shared in false confidence. In both cases the haters see it as a choice, and also in both cases the fact that the difference isn't visual contributes to the discrimination; the great power Jews and gay people share, the reason we're feared as much as we're hated, is that we have the potential to walk amongst you.

17 How many times have we heard from American politicians advocating for the Second Amendment that the Holocaust would've been averted if the Jews were armed, i.e. that it was Jews' fault for being victims?

to wait for a non-Jew, Quentin Tarantino, to invent Jewsploitation in *Inglourious Basterds*?) And where does this leave the Jews who want to play sports or stand up to oppression, like my cousin Max who was arrested for punching a Blackshirt on Ridley Road, a moment captured in a photo by Don McCullin?

Before Woody, my great Jewish hero was a character from a computer game who turned out to be a real-life wrestler called Goldberg. In the game he was undefeatable, a bald-headed, Speedo-clad superman whose finishing move started as a suplex but froze with his opponent upside down, fully extended like an exclamation mark while the blood drained from their legs, then somehow ended in a pin that was both brutal and balletic. For all the flexibility comedy allowed, these two ideas of Jewishness could not co-exist. How could we be both? And why was one accepted and the other exceptional, the exception that proved the rule?

Was there any part of being Jewish that could be understood outside the frame of our oppression?

Back to 2008 and, as had become our tradition and financial saving grace, my friend Darren and I were taking our latest play to the provincial arts centre in the suburban town where we'd both grown up. This time, though, things were different. While in the previous two years we'd needed this homecoming show to claw back some of the summer's losses, both fiscal and emotional, this year we'd actually had some success. We'd sold more than 90 per cent of the seats for our feature-length farce, compared to 50 per cent the year before, and had won by far our best reviews yet, including an actual rave from *The Stage* (whose wording, I'm embarrassed to admit, I still remember today). We were looking forward, then, to a glorious homecoming, a victory lap in front of the friendly crowd of family, friends and family friends that could usually be relied on to pack out the 300-seater auditorium on a week night when the rental rates were cheaper.

Owing to a complete lack of talent and an accompanying disdain for a craft I'd never possessed, I didn't act in the plays we wrote, so as ever I got to watch the room populate from my usual seat in the control booth. There, elevated over the crowd, I watched the rows fill with people I'd known most my life, faces so familiar I recognised most of them from the tops of their heads. As always it was flattering to see that they'd turned out to support us (and paid for the favour), but while in the first year the mood was dutiful, charity mixed with a healthy dose of dread, now there was an air of calmness, perhaps even anticipation. Clusters of friendly benefactors chatted amiably until the lights went down, when I saw three hundred phones light up, like a sudden vigil, then sync into black. I cued the first light cue and waited for the laughter to roll forward from the stage like one of Zigi's Rs. By now I knew where the laughs came and how long they lasted and tonight these would be bigger and there'd be some new laughs altogether. There was nothing a roomful of Jews liked more than laughing about another roomful of Jews.

But when the laughs did come they were brief and in pockets, and at the interval the applause was hesitant, muted. As I brought the house lights up, I knew something wasn't right. I vacated my vantage and went down to the foyer, ostensibly to get a drink but really to soak in the adulation I still residually expected, but no one would meet my eye. And when it was time to dim the lights again for the start of the second half, I spotted some empty seats.

The second half saw the introduction of Simon's brother, Andy, a defector to Christianity who'd been estranged from his parents to such an extent that they'd never met his four-year-old son, and while he riffed on his problems with Judaism and his mother in general, I saw people wince, heard some actual groans. They laughed generously at silly jokes about Bugs Bunny and *The Apprentice*, but when it came to the climactic reveal and Simon's relief to break free from the shackles of his Jewishness, liberating him from his latent guilt about marrying out, the only sound was the hum of the lights. In Edinburgh, to an audience of non-Jews, this had killed every night, but when the lights came up for good, after the perfunctory curtain call, the room emptied faster than a shiva at the end of the free food.

In *Nanette*, her miraculous 2017 stand-up special, the comedian Hannah Gadsby, who grew up gay in rural Tasmania, critiques the idea that self-deprecation is a marker of reclamation and self-empowerment. Rather, as she puts it, it's a mode the marginalised can speak in that allows them access to the world of their oppressors; the oppressed talks themself down as an act of supplication; 'to seek permission to speak'. This, to Gadsby, is a form of ritualised humiliation. In *Nanette* she rejects this humiliation, even if it means her career as a comedian is over.

Gadsby goes on to explain, with brutalising candour, the effect of growing up in a homophobic environment, one in which 70 per cent of the adults responsible for her care believed that homosexuals were a deviant subspecies: by the time she identified as gay, it was 'too late'; she was 'already homophobic'.

If our play about Jews was anti-Semitic it wasn't because we'd grown up surrounded by anti-Semites who believed we were less than human, it was because self-hatred, whether in the form of self-deprecation or self-erasure (all those Jewish comedies in which no one ever lit a candle or had two sets of forks) was the value we most strongly identified with in our idea of Jewishness. We weren't speaking in the language of our oppressor (no one had oppressed us), but in a language passed down to us from those who knew how to play to the gallery. Probably it was a matter of subtlety and execution. Jokes that play with harmful stereotypes and exaggerate negative traits play a dangerous game not because they can't be funny – the history of Jewish comedy shows us that they frequently are – but because you never know who could be listening and which part they might be laughing at.

By way of example: Moishe and Solly pass a Catholic church and see a sign that reads *Convert to Catholicism, $50 Cash.* Moishe turns to Solly and says, 'I think I'm going to give it a go.' He enters the church and returns a few minutes later. 'So, did you convert? What was it like?' asks Solly. 'It was nothing,' says Moishe. 'You go in, a guy sprinkles you with holy water and says "Congratulations, you're a Catholic."' 'So did you get the $50?' asks Solly. 'Is that all you people think about?' spits Moishe. Depending on where and how you laugh, you're a Jew or an anti-Semite, possibly both.

In other words, you can jump from the stool or wait for it to be kicked but either way you end up in the same predicament. And if all humour is gallows humour, something Jews understand better than most, you still have to decide which side of the gallows you're on, whose funeral you're attending.

There's a coda to the scene in *Anything Else* when Woody treats the thugs' car like a bonus level in *Street Fighter II*, in which Jason Biggs's character, a writer, sits alone in front of his computer trying to write up the events of the day while his wife sleeps next door.

Excitedly he turns to the camera and, couched by his hesitancy and his clinical assessment that the man is a 'psychotic lunatic', expresses his admiration for his mentor's act of revenge. In the face of injustice, he resisted. There are always those who will resist. And the issue, as Woody Allen playing the anti-Woody Allen tells his mentee, is 'always fascism'.

In 2004, in an arts cinema in Brighton, this was a good joke, but I read it now as a conversation across years. On the one side is a young nebbish, a pick-and-mix of inherited traumas and traits, who cowers from conflict and lives in prosperity, and on the other is an old man who's seen too much and understands that sometimes you don't need a quip or a self-directed comeback, you need a tyre iron.

Chapter Four:
Security

From the age of thirteen to eighteen I attended a fee-paying school just north of North London called Merchant Taylors', on a scholarship, I liked to claim. To get there I had to catch a coach from Radlett, the town I was brought up in, to the school's site in Northwood, a forty-minute drive away through the Jewish commuter belt of Borehamwood and Stanmore. Radlett, like every town where anyone's ever grown up, was strange and mundane in equal measure. Giant mock-Tudor mansions sat back from narrow lanes behind remote-controlled gates, and the fruit shop, where I had my first job, charged over the odds for fruit less shiny than you could buy from the supermarket. It had two synagogues and enough Jews to keep two Chinese restaurants (Tim's Table and Pang's Cottage) in business, all of these arranged on the Roman road that provided its high street and also housed the coach stop where each morning I waited for a green-striped Reynolds Diplomat with my friend Jon, who I knew from Hebrew class.

The coach arrived at seven thirty and left at seven thirty-five, but some mornings it was late, which was significant because it meant one of our friends from Hebrew school (who certainly I would prefer to remain nameless) would pass on the way to her bus stop a little further down the high street. Both Jon and I had an unbearable crush on our friend, which neither of us would confess to, so, in the way of teenage boys who are even more scared of acceptance than they are of rejection, we pretended we disliked her. Whenever our coach was late and we saw her walking towards us, thumbs hooked in the straps of her cello bag, we turned our backs and pretended to be deep in philosophical debate, or took cover in the Princess Diana commemorative garden that sloped down from the road. And so it was that at quarter to eight one Wednesday morning I boarded the coach without my games bag, which in my haste to avoid talking to someone I wanted to kiss I'd left on a bench next to the shelter.

It wasn't until break, so around eleven o'clock, that, with a sinking feeling in my gut, I realised I didn't have it and where I'd left it, where with any luck it still was. I didn't yet have a phone so I had to borrow Jon's to call my mum and ask if she could collect it. As luck would have it, she was running errands on the same street as the bus stop. But she was caught in traffic – there was some kind of incident and half the high street had been cordoned off. There were sirens sounding, lights flashing, policemen talking anxiously into their lapel-mounted radios. The word was that there was some kind of bomb threat. We realised at about the same time. My coach stop was opposite the Orthodox synagogue and my games bag, which I'd been given as a bar mitzvah present, was a nondescript black canvas hold-all, tastefully monogrammed and bulging with the trainers, towels and football boots I'd stuffed in it that morning.

For years I told this as a funny story. It was one of my most reliable, alongside the time I mistook Rachel Stevens from S Club 7 for a family friend, and the other time I accidentally micturated on a cat in Paris.[18] It was only much later that I started to consider

18 Ask me at a reading.

the underlying implications. The year before I left my sports bag at the bus stop, over three successive weekends in April, a neo-Nazi militant and former member of the BNP by the name of David Copeland had planted a series of nail bombs in Brixton, the East End and Soho. Collectively he'd been targeting the concept of plurality and specifically (respectively) London's black, South Asian and gay communities.

The first bomb was made using explosives from fireworks taped to the inside of a sports bag. It was detonated near the Iceland supermarket on Brixton Road, injuring forty-eight passers-by. The second bomb, again taped inside a sports bag, was meant to detonate at the Brick Lane street market that each Sunday attracted a large number of Bangladeshi locals, but scoring low for cultural awareness David had set it to go off on the Saturday and was unable to change the timer so it exploded in a less-crowded Hanbury Street, injuring thirteen and doing significant damage to surrounding buildings and cars. The third bomb, the most lethal, was detonated the day after my fourteenth birthday in the Admiral Duncan pub in Old Compton Street. It seriously injured seventy-nine people and killed three.

In response to these attacks, which police believed were triggered by the release of the Stephen Lawrence Inquiry,[19] synagogues across the country tightened security. Synagogues in London, as

---

19 Stephen Lawrence, for any too young to remember, was the black teenager murdered while waiting for a bus in South London by a gang of white teens, only two of whom were charged over twelve years later. The inquiry, officially known as the Macpherson Report, investigated claims that the Metropolitan Police had done little to apprehend his killers and were institutionally racist, a phrase the report coined. On its recommendation the double jeopardy rule was overturned, meaning two of the killers, who'd initially been acquitted, could be tried again for the crime.

far as I was aware, had always had security but mostly this meant volunteers armed with bushy eyebrows and questioning looks (on Yom Kippur my dad and my brother took turns), or wannabe commandos with wraparound Oakleys and one walkie-talkie between three, but for a short period police officers were assigned to stand guard outside some Saturday services. At the time this struck me as in pretty poor taste. It seemed paranoid, and not a little self-aggrandising, to lump ourselves in with someone else's tragedy. Unseemly because now wasn't the time to be thinking about ourselves but to be standing in solidarity with these communities in grieving. Paranoid because hating Jews had long since gone out of fashion, probably permanently, like cargo shorts or eyebrow bolts. If anything, here was proof even my parents couldn't deny that even neo-Nazis had higher priorities.

'Are you experiencing much anti-Semitism?' my grandpa Cyril, my dad's dad, would always ask when I visited on trips home from university. Always in the first five minutes of a conversation, while the tea was still too hot to sip. It was never *any*, always *much*. And how absurd was the presumption! I went to the University of Sussex and lived in Brighton, the most accepting place I'd ever been: men kissed in public and interracial couples walked down the street hand in hand, two things I'd almost never seen during my upbringing. And it was 2005, a good sixty years since everyone had pretty much agreed flat-out that hating Jews was a bad look. Of course, I understood where it came from. This was my grandfather whose parents had fled the pogroms at the end of the nineteenth century, who'd lived through the Nazis and the Blackshirts, who'd sent both his sons to a Jewish school where they were required to wear kippahs and on the way to which they'd been spat at and had stones thrown at them, so I did my best to humour him.

'Not too much,' I'd say, leaving the door ajar, throwing him a bone. I didn't tell him about the protests against Israel's treatment of the Palestinians, the boycott of Israeli goods from the union shops and the burning Star of David I'd walked past in the library square, because it had no relevance. Had the union been protesting Chinese or Syrian human rights abuses I wouldn't have told him that either. 'Not much,' I'd repeat, frowning as if racking my brain for something I might've forgotten: some pogrom or *Kristallnacht*.

He'd nod, looking troubled. Sunlight would catch in the dust motes that had escaped my grandma's daily hoover. The TV guide would wink up at me, the nightly news circled in red biro.

'And do you tell people you're Jewish?'

Sure. Usually I wasted little time. After so long identifying as lapsed, as soon as I'd arrived at university I'd started playing up to being Jewish. In part this was the contrarian streak I'd honed playing the Wicked Child at all those Seders, a contrarian streak that was at the centre of what I thought it meant to be Jewish, but mostly it was the need to have some identifying mark, something that would work as a placeholder until I figured out who I wanted to be. At school all my friends had been Jews. We'd been the Jew Crew, a name we'd either coined or readily adopted. At weekends we went to Jewish parties, where Jewish teenagers shuffled past Jewish bouncers and drank Jewish fizzy drinks and danced to drum 'n' bass, waiting for the drop like accountants waiting for April.

But at university, away from the suburbs of North London, for the first time I was the only Jew in the room. In many cases, the first Jew people were meeting, at least knowingly. It was a surprise to many that I didn't have the curly sideburns and the furry tyre hat, but to compensate I talked at length about *Seinfeld*, occasionally said 'oy' and read a lot of Philip Roth (the whole Zuckerman Bound trilogy, including *The Prague Orgy*). I made lots of jokes about my grandparents' cooking and how my mum had taken us to strangers' funerals for the practice, and I encouraged jokes from others. My housemates found it funny to talk about stolen gold and answer everything I said with a question ('You want I should open the window?'), and so did I. I'd long ago lapsed on the dietary front (those first watery rashers in the school canteen, pale and wrinkly like the skin under a plaster) but I made it a matter of pride to gorge myself on prawn curries and BLTs: not all Jews, I explained, were bound by ancient laws that might've made sense once when we lived in the desert, but had been obsolete since the invention of the cool box. I saw myself, in part, I suppose, as an ambassador. Jewish people, it was my job to demonstrate, were just like you. We were just funnier and had better hair.

I never encountered anything I considered anti-Semitic (a friend's girlfriend, on learning I was Jewish, once insisted I watch *Life Is Beautiful* but even after borrowing it from the library I failed to take offence), certainly nothing I'd have thought to report to my grandpa. Meanwhile I developed an interest in politics. I came from a privileged background in which politics was rarely discussed – in which people had the privilege to consider themselves apolitical, which is like believing that you don't have an accent – and for the first time in my life I was being exposed to people whose backgrounds didn't resemble mine in the slightest. Sussex was a hotbed of progressive politics, activism and debate and it was invigorating to confront the extent of my own ignorance. Every week there was a protest in favour of or against something I'd not previously heard of: the Kondovo Crisis, the Kivu Conflict, the Climate Apocalypse. There were groups dedicated to all of these and the Students' Union had an official stance on most, and while I didn't join any groups, I reported on them for the union paper and slowly began to develop a vocabulary of inequality and injustice.

I read about genocides in Rwanda and Indonesia and took a free trial of LoveFilm to rent the first two discs of *Roots*. I didn't actually watch it – the DVD player on my laptop was stuck on the wrong region from my imported copies of *The Larry Sanders*

Show – but I read up on the Atlantic slave trade and the war in the Balkans and in a rare foray into the library I got lost on my way to Cognitive Linguistics and, despite having an essay due, spent several hours learning about Pol Pot and the Khmer Rouge. I sometimes wonder now if this newfound interest in ethnic cleansing and racial atrocity was a way of confronting something a little closer to home – the way we watch an eclipse through its reflection on a lake – but if you'd asked me at the time I'd have dismissed the suggestion with no little anger. Not everything was about being Jewish. That was the one thing I had no interest in learning about because it was the one thing in which I was already an expert. At best, perhaps my Jewishness informed some morbid fascination that was tangentially related to my new reading list, but this was non-definitive and clutching at straws.

And then one night in my second year, living off-campus in a flat above a fish shop, I stumbled back from the pub and found my much drunker housemate watching *The Boys from Brazil* on our giant bulbous fish tank of a TV. Probably if I'd had the head for some Ralph Ellison or Cornel West I wouldn't have settled next to him on the fake leather sofa and let the film flicker over me, but I did. The plot, as far as I could piece together (this was the now-alien experience of being airdropped into a film's second act and having to tunnel out in two directions at once), concerned a secret organisation of former Nazi war criminals, and a twitchy former Auschwitz physician who, for reasons that started off vague but quickly revealed themselves as bonkers, was intent on assassinating ninety-four far-flung sixty-year-olds, all of whom were cruel fathers to adopted sons. All ninety-four of these adopted sons had been born in the sixties to surrogate mothers who had been fertilised using zygotes carrying a preserved strand of Hitler's DNA. Each of these children had then been placed in foster homes that mimicked the conditions of Hitler's upbringing, and were now being activated by the murder of their fathers at the same age that Hitler had lost his.

As plots went it felt like something that been dreamed up as an end-of-year finale by an Adderall-addled intern in a professional wrestling writers' room, and this was matched by the execution, which was sloppy, kitschy and badly acted. I was astonished to learn in the end credits that I'd been watching Laurence Olivier and Gregory Peck in a script based on a book by Ira Levin, who'd also written *The Stepford Wives* and *Rosemary's Baby*. In places it was so unintentionally arch it was almost comedy: a sort of *Carry on Kampfing*. But somehow – perhaps the lateness of the hour – the film burrowed its way into the grey matter of my brain and the deeper tissue of my subconscious. The character played by Olivier was an ailing Viennese Nazi hunter, a phrase I'd never before heard and which struck me as inherently absurd, like *brainchild*, and I was staggered to learn, also in the closing credits, that he'd been based on a real-life figure: Simon Wiesenthal.

A survivor himself, Simon Wiesenthal had died just a few months earlier at the age of ninety-six in his adopted home of Vienna after a life dedicated to bringing escaped Nazi war criminals to justice. Just three years earlier, in 2002, the centre named for him and his semi-legendary exploits (it was acting on information provided by Wiesenthal that Israeli authorities were ultimately able to apprehend Adolf Eichmann in Buenos Aires in 1960) had launched an initiative called Operation Last Chance that appealed for information on the long list of ex-Nazis they still suspected of living in hiding; the operation was so-named because the Nazis it sought were approaching the ends of their lives and so would otherwise evade justice.[20]

---

20 Nine years later, in 2011, with comic chops that almost but don't quite soften the blow, they would launch Operation Last Chance 2.

That this should stagger me made little logical sense, but it shook me to foundations I didn't know I had. Of course, I knew there were survivors – I'd always known this – but I'd never considered the other end of the equation: that there were still Nazis. This was a different thought entirely. Nazis had always been history's bogeymen, so anachronistic they were almost mythic. You half expected them to be ten foot tall with laser vision and detachable jaws. They were the sort of story parents told young children to get them to bed or promote good oral health: *Brush your teeth or the Nazis will get you!* Even with everything I knew about the destruction they had wrought, even with the ways it had already impacted my family's life, they felt less like historical fact than rhetorical device.

And yet here was a centre dedicated to tracking them down in 2002! There were Nazis with Yahoo addresses. Nazis on Friendster. Nazis in cargo pants and sleeveless flannel shirts.

I knew a little about the sanctions they'd faced and the justice they'd evaded – Hitler in the bunker; the Nuremberg trials; Eichmann in a suit and tie, scribbling notes inside a bulletproof box – but only now did I start to read up. What had happened to the perpetrators of one of the greatest crimes against humanity that had ever been committed?

The answer, it seemed, was not much. At the end of the war the US, the UK and the Soviet Union had formed a temporary executive body, the Allied Control Council, to rule over an occupied Germany, and from January 1946 had set themselves the task of ridding its culture, workforce and judiciary of any vestige of National Socialist ideology, a process known as denazification. Quickly, though, the scale of the task became evident. During and before the war around eight and a half million Germans had been members of the Nazi party, with another forty-plus million belonging to Nazi affiliates, like the Hitler Youth and the German Labour

Front. Once the Council had abandoned the Morgenthau Plan (which proposed reducing Germany's industrial capacity to the level of subsistence farming), it was forced to confront the fact that Germany would be unable to rebuild its economy if every person with Nazi ties faced prosecution.

Meanwhile, the Americans in particular had become victims of their early enthusiasm. In the first few months of Allied occupation, when the eyes of the world's media were trained on the Council's headquarters in Berlin, US authorities had required all German citizens over the age of eighteen to answer a questionnaire on their memberships, activities and movements during the Third Reich. The idea was to place them all into one of five categories – Major Offenders, Offenders, Lesser Offenders, Followers and Exonerated Persons – but the main result was that the troops charged with processing the data were soon buried under an avalanche of paperwork.

By the end of 1945 over seven million former Nazis still awaited classification, which triggered a change in policy: denazification was to continue as a top priority of the occupation, but now would concentrate on removing the physical symbols of Nazism (no more swastikas or Adolf Hitler Avenues) and on the German high command – those who hadn't long since fled – who would face trial at Nuremberg, where eleven Nazis were sentenced to death.[21]

By the start of 1946, American newspapers had stopped calling for justice for the Jews of Europe and started calling instead for the return home of troops who'd been left behind to process questionnaires. By March, the US withdrew from the investigation completely, handing over its preliminary findings to an interim German judiciary comprised of former Nazis, Nazi affiliates and individuals still yet to be classified. (I had to read this several times.) The Germans stuck with the Americans' original five classifications and

---

21   None had been sentenced to death before nor have been since.

concentrated on streamlining their investigations by, among other measures: issuing blanket exemptions; downgrading verdicts to avoid trial; issuing fines in now-worthless deutschmarks; admitting into evidence the testimonies of the accused's friends and families (the so-called *Persilscheine*, named after the detergent, known for its stain-removing qualities); and turning a blind eye to the rampant black market for the forgery and sale of denazification certificates, so that by 1948, through a combination of collusion, corruption and bureaucratic malfeasance, hundreds of thousands, maybe millions, of Nazis had been quietly folded back into German society.

Which was not to say the world had lost interest in Nazis altogether. Back in 1945, while the Allied Control Council had been gathering questionnaires and renaming roads, the US military had launched Operation Paperclip, the second-most tenacious and thorough search for high-ranking Nazis ever conducted by a foreign government. Over the next fifteen years, over 1,600 scientists, engineers, strategists and technicians were spirited from Nazi Germany to the US, where they were exonerated, rehoused without personal expense and set to work on American military strategy or aeronautics. I'd always wondered how Dr. Strangelove (*né* Merkwürdigliebe) had come to occupy such an exalted position in Merkin Muffley's war council, and now I knew.

Meanwhile, on the other side of the Space Race, the Soviets had conducted their own Operation Osoaviakhim, which had recruited more than two thousand former Nazis and moved them to the Soviet Union with their partners and families.

◆ ◆ ◆

But so what? All of this was vaguely upsetting but it was ancient history and had no relevance to my life in Sussex and my grandparents' in Middlesex. Yes, it was jarring that in a very real sense the Nazis had escaped recrimination for what they'd done to my family and the families of my friends, but on a practical, pragmatic level it said nothing to my safety; that there were still Nazis and that they were hiding in plain sight did not make me any less safe or my family any less paranoid. The last thing a Nazi in hiding would do was blow his cover by exhuming old habits.

And anti-Semitism, the idea that someone would hate Jews, seemed no less anachronistic. I still didn't understand why we needed gates on our community centres and guards outside our temples. Never in my life had I felt unsafe because I was Jewish. Once some friends and I had been set upon by a gang of men in motorcycle helmets. One head-butted me (I've still got the scar on my forehead) while some others bundled my friend Rob into an alley and threw some punches and kicks. All of us were Jewish and the area we were walking in had a long Jewish history but there was no way our attackers could have known this. None of us *looked* Jewish, whatever that meant. And they hadn't taken any-thing, which proved the attack was random, the only motive the lack of motive. In 2004 a Nazi was someone who corrected grocers' apostrophes or refused you service in their pop-up restaurant. (It hadn't yet acquired another of its current definitions: *someone you don't agree with*.) Past trauma was exactly that: traumatic but in the past.

It's not like there were Nazis in Edgware or enrolling as mature students on linguistics courses in East Sussex. So when my grandpa asked me again the next time I went home if I was experiencing much anti-Semitism, I was less reserved, more effusive. No, none. I never had. And now I understood what he was really asking. For a certain generation, anti-Semitism was central to their concep-tion of Jewish identity which, like mine, had been forged in child-hood. My grandfather needed it, needed to believe in it as a way of understanding his Jewishness. And he needed *me* to believe in it as a means to relate to my experience.

And perhaps in a broader sense Jewishness needed it too. Perhaps we needed moats round our cultural centres and police outside our shuls as a way to convince ourselves that the threat was ongoing. Because we needed an excuse for failing to integrate fully into a society that didn't see us as different. Because if we didn't believe in God we needed something to organise around. Maybe we enjoyed being ghettoised so much that we'd done it to ourselves.

◆ ◆ ◆

My older brother, the Wise Child, now works as a teacher in a Jewish primary school and has this to say on the subject of security:

'By eight or nine the kids are very aware of anti-Semitism. We do intruder drills once a term. We start at age four. When the alarm sounds the children know to move away from windows and external doors so they can't be viewed from outside. Some schools make a game of it – they call it Sleeping Lions – but we just make them sit on the floor in silence; we don't want them thinking it's a game because it's not. We do these drills a few times each year, at various times in the school day. There are drills to get them all inside if they're out in the playground, contingencies if there's a group out on a school trip – how are we going to communicate with them to ensure they don't come into a potentially dangerous situation? What to do if there are four hundred kids inside and twenty left on the playground. We vary the assembly points in case one becomes unsafe. We also have evacuation procedures in place in case of bomb threats – several have been made against Jewish schools in the last few years. All Jewish schools have security and the site is swept a couple of times a day.'

In 2015, in Paris, in the wake of the *Charlie Hebdo* shootings, a gunman entered a kosher supermarket and took nineteen Jewish hostages.[22] He murdered four of them before he was killed himself by French police. Did security heighten after such a targeted attack?

'No. I mean, look at Toulouse[23] or the attacks in Nice.[24] Or more recently look at Pittsburgh.[25] We've been doing security for years. We have regular briefings from CST [the Community Security Trust, a charity that provides security advice and training to Jewish communal organisations, schools and synagogues] . . . There's a governor whose responsibility is security . . . We're lucky that we've got a secure site and we tweaked our security arrangements accordingly because after each drill there's an assessment about what needs to change, if there are things we need to adapt . . . Jewish schools all have security guards. They all have gates. Other schools are waking up to the risks of terrorism now but we've been used to this for years. It's been normalised for a very long time.'

So what does he say to accusations that the Jewish community is cossetted, that it hides behind walls of its own making, and that this separatism breeds a natural suspicion from those outside of

---

22 Three years later, on the anniversary of the siege, the supermarket, which had since been defaced with swastikas, burned down in a suspected arson attack.

23 In March 2012, four days after shooting two off-duty French soldiers, a gunman targeted staff and pupils at a Jewish day school, killing a teacher and three children, aged four, five and seven.

24 In February 2015, three soldiers patrolling a Jewish community centre were stabbed by a lone assailant. In 2016, on Bastille Day, a terrorist drove a truck into crowds of revellers on the Promenade des Anglais, killing eighty-six people – in this case the targets weren't specifically Jewish.

25 In October 2018, a far-right terrorist stormed a synagogue during a Shabbat service and opened fire, killing eleven people; we'll return to this later.

them? At this question, the Wise Child – now thirty-five – sighs. 'I've had conversations with non-Jewish friends who are shocked that there're security guards outside shuls and Jewish schools. Both in terms of "Why the fuck do you need it?" and "It's ridiculous that you do need it." When I've been on security at shul I've often had complaints from members of the public about how we are shutting ourselves off from wider society. In school we explicitly foster a sense of dual identity: Jewish identity and a British identity. We're very explicit that we're proud British Jews: we're proud British people and we're proud Jewish people. And the two strands of identity are intertwined and both strands are a key component of what we teach . . . But there's always a balance to be struck between being public-facing and a community hub, and being aware of the heightened risks, and most people you speak to fall somewhere along that spectrum. No one wants to build ten-foot walls with barbed wire and CCTV but to be completely open increases the risk; it's a big conversation that people are having . . . It's easy to normalise things that it takes an outside view to realise are a bit strange or extreme, and it's true that as a community and as individuals we live behind barriers, but you only have to look at the things that have happened in France, in Belgium,[26] in Turkey,[27] in Denmark.[28] As a Jewish community we're aware that we're on the list . . . We try not to be complacent.'

26 In May 2014, in Brussels, a gunman opened fire on the Jewish Museum of Belgium, killing four people.
27 The Neve Shalom Synagogue in Istanbul has been the target of three separate terror attacks since 1986. Anti-Semitism in Turkey has its own Wikipedia page with a subsection dedicated to 'Violence against Jews'.
28 In February 2015, a gunman interrupted a bar mitzvah ceremony taking place at the Great Synagogue in central Copenhagen, firing nine rounds and killing a community member who was on security duty.

◆ ◆ ◆

When we talk about assimilation what we're talking about is security, and when we talk about security what we're talking about is assimilation. My grandfather himself, who was worried – I realise now – that away at university I would lose touch with or give up my Jewish identity, changed the family name from Greenbaum to Greene on entering the navy since he understood the importance of not standing out from the crowd. (I've always wondered about that final, superfluous *e*, a ghost of something abandoned, silent but not weightless.)

But what does it mean to assimilate to a culture? For one it's based on an assumption that increasingly fails to hold: that we can (or should) calculate difference from some mythical, monocultural baseline. In a pluralist society, *assimilation*, which always sounds negative, or at least bittersweet (the initial sibilance making it sound like someone slipping out of something, shedding a skin), would not be a word we'd need in our vocabulary since every contact between cultures would be a two-way exchange that led to mutual enrichment. But while in recent years we've made strides towards certain forms of pluralism, it's the mythical baseline that most often prevails. The expectation remains on the smaller culture to assimilate to the larger, to adopt its ideals and sand down what edges don't fit to its mould. This becomes the price of entry: standing out in any way, whether through your dress or the gates round your temples, breeds resentment and sometimes hostility. (Look how similarly right-wing commentators couch their Islamophobic views in the language of openness, accusing women in burqas of closing themselves off, as if from a society that would otherwise embrace them.) It makes assimilation both a failure and a requirement and asks only in return that you adopt the specifically British values of openness and tolerance, which means being open to closed-mindedness and tolerant of intolerance, even if they're being directed towards your own community; it's the height of bad manners to point this out.

But this all supposes assimilation is a conscious undertaking rather than what naturally happens when you're part of a community who've lived uneventfully enough alongside others for more than a hundred years; that Jewish life is some alien culture that needs weaving into the fabric of British society and is not already an integral part of it. I had two great-grandfathers who fought for Britain in the First World War, so why, in 2005, was I worried about self-ghettoisation?

◆ ◆ ◆

'Why Not Intermarry? *It's forbidden by the Torah! You're finishing Hitler's work!'* So begins an article published on aish.com. The italicised parts (the italics are the site's own) are tongue-in-cheek, but from a tactical rather than logical standpoint. These are common negative arguments and are rarely effective. A better approach, the article suggests, is 'the rational, practical view'.

The article goes on to outline a series of obstacles to interfaith marriage and relationships. It references a young Jewish woman describing the precarious state of her marriage after her (non-Jewish) husband objects to circumcising their newborn son, resulting in crippling doubts and 'terrible fights'. It cites Egon Mayer, a professor at Brooklyn College, who explains that intermarriages have higher divorce rates because when one party suppresses something as important as their religious identity, it becomes a 'time bomb'. It quotes the famed relationship therapist (and Belgian Jew) Esther Perel. The tension isn't between two religions but in differing attitudes on a variety of issues, from food to sex, from modes of parenting to 'styles of emotional expressiveness . . . all of [which] are culturally embedded'.

In other words, intermarriage (and its avoidance) is not an ethical or romantic question but one of pragmatism and insurance – or, as the article explicitly states (under the advisory heading 'Take a Break'), the belief that love will overcome is erroneous and a sign that one is merely infatuated. A good marriage is built on shared goals and cultural assumptions, without which 'love will dissipate'. For anyone considering intermarriage, it suggests a three-month trial separation. Failing this, couples should at least agree to three months without physical contact. Finally, as if it's not yet shown its hand, the article quotes a Rabbi Kalman Packouz, 'author of [the book] *How to Prevent an Intermarriage*'.

Aish is an Orthodox Jewish outreach organisation considered extreme by many Jews both in its religious observance and its recruitment of Jews from less- and non-religious backgrounds (families will sometimes talk of losing children to Aish, or of them being *aished*). But versions of this view – that intermarriage is to be avoided or at best tolerated – are common and filter down through several strata of Jewish cultural belief. Not everyone maintains that marrying out is finishing Hitler's work but there are many, including my grandmother, who would openly prefer that their children and grandchildren married Jews. Recently my cousin announced her engagement and it was remarked on, immediately and admiringly, that she was the first of our generation to find a Jewish partner.

◆　◆　◆

My son's full name is Arthur Elijah Greene, so named, I like to joke, because *Jew* didn't scan. It wasn't until my second year in Sussex that I met Imogen, my partner and Arthur's mother, at a New Year's

Eve party at her house and then, the following week, in a seminar for an elective few enough people had chosen for it to feel like fate. Pretty soon we were spending every hour outside lectures in each other's company – and every night on the floor-mounted mattress we generously pretended was an aesthetic choice.

Imogen wasn't Jewish – still isn't. She was from Devon, which was like not being Jewish but more so. Both of her parents were churchgoers but since Christianity is more opt-in than opt-out it didn't follow that she was Christian herself. Rather, she was nothing. A free agent. Like all nominal white Christians, she could break down her heritage into ever-decreasing fractions – a quarter Dutch, a sixteenth Irish – and she'd never met a Jew, or not knowingly, until the year before when she'd arrived at Sussex, but her mum taught secondary school RE and she knew as much as I did, maybe more, about Jewish festivals and practices – not that they had much to do with my idea of Jewishness.

After a few weeks together Imogen and I were an item, and after a few months we'd agreed to stay together the following year when she moved to France for her studies. This was already the longest and most committed relationship I'd ever been in (I still have a prepaid phone) and we were in love in a way that if it wasn't magic was some pretty convincing sleight of hand. So it was a surprise when she returned to Brighton from a visit home with a change of expression, a sudden pre-emptive aloofness. I asked what was wrong. She'd had a conversation with her mum.

'Are you going to break up with me because I'm not Jewish?'

I laughed and assured her the question was absurd – if anyone was breaking up with anyone it was Imogen with me when she found out how cranky I got if I had less than eight hours' sleep or how often I repeated the story about the time I'd mistaken Rachel from S Club for a family friend. But incubated in the airlock of her mind, the question had grown from a vague hypothesis to a near-certainty.

'What about if we have kids? Wouldn't you want to raise them Jewish?'

I laughed again. We were twenty years old. I'd never thought about having kids. *We* were kids. If we had kids I'd want to raise them in the same way they were conceived: rhetorically. But Imogen, always more advanced than I was, insisted. I'd told her, on one of our early dates, about my great-aunt who'd been disowned by my great-grandma for marrying someone who wasn't Jewish, and while I'd told her this with great disdainful irony, purely to illustrate my family's dysfunction, was it possible I'd had some ulterior motive? Being Jewish might not have meant much to me at twenty but people changed. Who was to say it wouldn't become important in the future. And if it did, wouldn't I rather be with someone Jewish just in case?

I laughed again and dismissed the premise of the question – I wanted to be with Imogen – but it bounced back, retooled and reloaded: 'Wouldn't you rather *I* was Jewish?'

Years later, in a novel about lapsed Jewish identity, before I scrapped it and folded it into the book you're reading, I wrote the following interaction between the protagonist, Ezra, and his heavily pregnant non-Jewish wife, Lucy. They were at an NCT class, going round the circle, introducing themselves to the group:

> *'This is Lucy,' I offered, meekly. 'She grew up in a house without an inside toilet, we're having a boy, and sorry, what was the third thing?'*
>
> *'A family tradition you're looking forward to continuing,' the instructor prompted.*

I tried to think of something innocuous. 'Well, he's a boy,
so I guess there's having him circumcised.'

There was a second's silence, the sort that you measure in
depth, not length. It was broken by Lucy laughing beside
me. 'He's joking,' she assured the circle.

'I'm serious,' I said, and only saying so realised it was true.

Sometimes it takes a perceptive outsider to articulate something you're not able to see. Looking back, I can see that Imogen was already braced for something I hadn't started to consider. And what she was really asking, I understand now, is a question about assimilation. I abhorred – still abhor – the view that presents intermarriage as an existential threat to Jews, that necessarily views non-Jews with an element of suspicion, and worries about dilution as if our blood is syrup; but at the same time I'm suspicious of the opposite view that sees assimilation teleologically, as a desirable endpoint, some modern-day promised land that means an end to all suffering through invisibility.

Back in 2006, certainly, I didn't see it as anything. It was neither the prize nor the price, just one in a series of presuppositions. And since my Jewishness was at best an inflection, it was also the premise for any nascent sense of identity I might be exploring. In my family and in my Jewish community I was only defined by what I wasn't (interested, observant), but in the wider world I was free to decide what my Jewishness meant. Without assimilation I was kosher for Passover chocolate: unappealing to everyone. With it I was kosher for Passover ketchup: the same but different.

Without assimilation I was (am?) barely a Jew.

I didn't say any of this to Imogen since I was still a decade and a half from thinking it. Instead I kissed her and told her I loved her, that I wouldn't want to change her in any way, and that I reserved the right to write about this in ten to fifteen years' time. I'm not sure she was convinced at first but I spent the rest of my twenties trying to prove it, and now, safely ensconced in the middle of our thirties, I think she's coming round to believing me.

Which, I suppose, is the one main difference between security and assimilation. One is a choice that for the most part is made for you, and the other, while also being something that can still be revoked, requires, in the first instance, some perseverance on your part.

Chapter Five:
Israel

When I was sixteen, in the summer of 2001, I went to Israel, for the first and last time in my life, with a Jewish youth group. We spent a month there, travelling the country by coach, sleeping in hostels, in kibbutzim, under stars and on rolled-up sweatshirts against rattling windows. The idea of the trip, so our leaders repeatedly reminded us, was that we would fall in love with the country, experience its spectacular variety and maybe establish or uncover some latent spiritual connection. Here, in no particular order, are some recollections:

> Dedicating the entire front pocket of my JanSport backpack to Wrigley's spearmint gum to ensure my breath would be minty fresh at all times, as unlike my school the tour was co-ed.

> Attempting to bleach my hair, misreading the instructions, and spending the whole summer with a luminous-orange nest on top of my head.

Listening to *Is This It* by The Strokes for the first time on cassette through the coach's ancient sound system, the only alternative to the much more popular Britney Spears and Destiny's Child.

Sharing a dorm room with a contestant on the original *Pop Idol*, who lived under the constant request to sing 'Affirmation' by Savage Garden.

Kissing a girl in a water park, noticing the imprint one of the cups of her bikini had made against my T-shirt and wondering if I'd discovered a new base (the furthest I'd ever got to).

Writing terrible poetry and desperately trying to share it with anyone who would listen.

Trying to smoke a 'spliff' rolled from the pages of a friend's diary and filled with a leaf one of our Israeli guards, who bore a thin resemblance to Jeff Bridges in *The Big Lebowski*, was always picking for tea.

Participating in an unofficial *Seinfeld*-inspired masturbation moratorium, which a friend from school who'd probably prefer to remain anonymous crashed out of, Kramer-style, on the flight over.

A McDonald's with a kosher menu.

My first taste of hummus.

There are other things I remember but they're hazier, composite images, averages taken from numerous effortful trawls. I remember visiting the Western Wall, the holiest religious site for Jews around the world, and feeling nothing besides the paralysing requirement to Feel Something, like a thousand New Year's Eves rolled into one. I remember waking before dawn to trek up a mountain to see the sunrise from Masada, the site of a mass suicide following a siege at the end of the first Jewish–Roman War. I also remember the insides of seminar rooms where we watched plays about Jewish oppression or, on one occasion, listened to a man with a stand-up's patter expose the anti-Israel bias in news reports from the BBC about the Conflict – the *C* always sounded capitalised. At the time, he struck me as suspect, but not through any political leaning; at sixteen you could've put me in a room with Aristotle and I'd have come out claiming he was a chancer.

It's the first set of recollections that present themselves most readily if I think about Israel, which unless forced to I rarely do, but the second set, along with other ideas, words, images that have attached themselves over the years, are what come to me if I think a little longer. Spiritually, my relationship with Israel is much like my relationship with Beyoncé, in that I don't have one, but no Jew can get too far before they're forced to engage with Israel in one form or the other.

So what are my views on Israel? Before we go any further, so no one feels misled, I should probably nail my colours to the mast.

My main view, the one I hold most vociferously and the only one I'd be confident debating to defend, is that I resent telling you. The obligation to have an opinion (namely, the correct opinion) about Israel is a stick often used to beat Jews in the diaspora, and in the absence of a statement, an opinion is assumed for us: any

Jew who doesn't explicitly state otherwise (and many who do) is a Zionist – a word whose meaning is so contested it makes you wonder if two people are ever really having the same conversation, or whether the whole of human history isn't a series of increasingly fraught, *Frasier*-style misunderstandings. Though, ironically, it is a word that tends to end debate.

But then, I suppose, on this one occasion no one asked, and you've stuck with me this far, so perhaps I can trust you with a little more.

First then, some history. The personal kind: the only kind that, when it comes to Israel, I'm qualified to speak to. Like, I suppose, many diasporic Jews my first awareness of a Jewish homeland was as a biblical reference, in the prayers we recited each year at the Seder table (right after the types of four children): *Eretz Yisrael . . . L'Shana Haba'ah*. Next year in Jerusalem. Israel, as I understood it, was where Jews came from, like a spawning point in a computer game. (Although not our type of Jews; we were European – or Ashkenazi – which meant we were from the shtetls, which was something else I didn't understand.) That it was a country that still existed today was evident from the globe we had at the front of our primary school classroom, but also surprising, like finding out your great-aunt knew how to beatbox. The two things were hard to reconcile, the biblical and the contemporary – I never thought of the two as points on the same line – but there it was: a clearly-defined landmass; a name on a departures board; the birthplace of Eyal Berkovic; an inexplicable contestant in Eurovision. Like many thirteen-year-old Jews, I'd bet, I felt a strange sense of pride when Dana International won the world's most politically sensitive sequin convention with 'Diva' in 1998, just as I'd felt two years earlier when Berkovic scored two past Peter Schmeichel in his debut season at Southampton. But it wasn't the type of pride you felt at the achievement of a loved one, more the kind you felt when an actor you'd once served in a pub was nominated for a lifetime achievement at the British Soap Awards.

Israel, like the rest of my Jewish identity, was a secret I kept from everyone who assumed I was just like them. But it was the sort of banal secret you kept without meaning to; it just wasn't interesting. No one in my family ever talked about Israel so I didn't know there was anything to talk about. Certainly not that it was something you could be pro or against. It just *was*.

It wasn't until my bar mitzvah, as coincidence would have it the week after Eurovision '98, that this view was first clouded with confusion. As a gift from the congregation, on completing my portion of the ceremony, I was presented with a book called *Israel at 50*. I didn't think much of it at first since I was far too busy with my other presents – a Swiss army knife, a shockproof Walkman, a stereo with a six-disc changer – and it would never have occurred to me to read it. But its spine stared down at me from the bookshelf above my bed until slowly I started to wonder. Fifty seemed awfully young for a country. I had cousins who were older than this. The football team I supported had been founded in 1905. In school we'd been reading a story called *Train to Rhodesia* but it still hadn't dawned on me that countries and their names weren't geological facts but the ebbing tidemarks of conflict and conquest. History and geography, as I understood them, were separate subjects, with different classrooms, textbooks and teachers. And it seemed particularly young for a country we sang about in our prayers, in a language that had *ancient* in its actual name.

Still, I wasn't curious enough to ask any questions or to crack the spine of the book that's probably still sitting, in pristine condition, in the bottom of a box in my grandparents' garage, or even to do any basic maths. I still hadn't heard the word *Palestine* (I'm not sure I had when I went to Jerusalem, although I did know there was a conflict, that there were streets it wasn't safe to walk down and that some of my friends' parents had deemed the whole trip too dangerous to send their kids on), but I'd moved from a state of blanket acceptance to one that fostered the conditions for curiosity: a sort of pre-curiosity. So I was primed for the next year when I first encountered the concept of Schrödinger's country and the illegal occupation.

As I remember it, though possibly erroneously (some of the detail is suspiciously specific), I was leaving the Harlequin Centre in Watford after a mortifying hour's shopping for new trainers with my mum when we passed a small group of protesters gathered round the fountain outside Accessorise. They were helmed, I seem to remember, by a woman with pink dreadlocks and a loudhailer, who now that I think of it bears an uncanny resemblance to someone I was at uni with, and who was attempting to gather signatures for a petition against the Zionist occupation of somewhere called the West Bank. I was several strides behind my mum, having no doubt paused to tie and retie the laces of the new trainers she'd generously bought me, and possibly I lingered (to reassert my independence and put some more distance between us) long enough to catch the word *apartheid*, which I'd learned from my sister a few weeks earlier in reference to South Africa. Another protester skipped towards me and thrust a clipboard into my hands. On it was a petition with a page or so of signatures. It called for the right of Palestinians to self-govern.

Before I could ask what Palestinians were or what it meant to self-govern, the girl with the loudhailer explained to anyone in earshot: Israel was an illegitimate state built on land stolen from its indigenous people on a scale unprecedented in all of human history.

Not surprisingly this came as a surprise. It seemed odd that no one had mentioned it before. At this point Mum was out of sight so I had no way to verify what the woman was telling me, but if it was true it felt like a sizeable omission, especially considering what I did know about the Aborigines and the Native Americans.

The other protester continued, holding out a pen. They were asking UK supermarkets to boycott all Israeli-made products until Israel agreed to tear down the settlements and end the illegal occupation.

'Right,' I probably said. 'Sure.'

The woman with the loudhailer refused to stand by while Israel violated the rights of a third of its population and meanwhile our government stood by and did nothing.

'Cool, gotcha.'

This was a lot of new information to process and for a moment I wondered if I'd misheard. Israel did what now? Were there two Israels?

I don't remember if I signed the petition – my guess would be I didn't because I was nervous about giving my name out – but back in the car I was moved to ask. What had the woman meant by an 'illegal occupation'?

Mum probably sighed before answering, sadly, 'Not everyone believes the Jews have a right to a homeland.'

Why not?

'Because they think we're safe where we are.'

And weren't we?

'Well, do you feel like you are?'

I thought about it. But for no more than a couple of chevrons. Of course I did. We lived in the suburbs of North London, the suburbs of suburbia, where the most exciting thing that had ever happened – this was before the bomb scare – was a recall of Creme Eggs from the local Budgens.

'Yes.'

'Good. OK then.'

'Why? Should I not?'

'Of course not, sweetie. Don't worry, nothing's going to happen to you.'

Later that evening, after dinner, as we were stacking the dishwasher, I asked my dad the same question. He jutted his bottom lip like a cash register then sighed, sadly too. 'The thing about being Jewish is you always need to be vigilant. If you think you're safe, you're probably being complacent. That's why we need a Jewish state, so there's somewhere we can go if the shit ever hits the fan again.'

This, of course, was insane. The idea that we might move from the Home Counties to the Middle East because the former was too dangerous! That my dad, who made us wear our seat belts until the key was out of the ignition, or my mum, who caked us in factor 50 on the first day of spring and spent holidays marshalling us between coins of shade, would uproot us to Israel, from where news footage looked like B-roll from an action film, because Hertfordshire wasn't safe. And what had the woman meant by Israel being an illegal state built on stolen land?

Dad rolled his eyes and left a chip pan to soak. 'They mean Jews are different. No one questions French people's right to live in France, or Spanish people's right to live in Spain. But with Jews it's a big debate.'

For a moment this sounded reasonable. But only a moment. 'But Jews aren't from Israel.'

'Of course we are! We're the Canaanites! We're the ancient Hebrews! Why the hell do you think they call us *Israelites*? Leave that, it's got to soak.'

I did leave it, the pan and the conversation. Until the next afternoon, on the drive to the all-Jewish football league I played in each Sunday. If there had always been Jews in Israel, who were the indigenous people the protesters had been talking about?

'The Arabs.'

Now I was more confused than ever. And finally I did the maths: 1998 minus 50. So what had been there before 1948? By this point I knew the creation of Israel, the one the book's title referred to, had something to do with the Holocaust, that it had been bequeathed to the Jews as some kind of recompense and future insurance, but I'd never considered what had been there before. It was too much to assume the UN had a spare country just knocking around, even if it was mostly desert. 'So the Arabs were there before the Jews?'

Dad shook his head and blared his horn at a dawdling Micra. 'There have been Jews in Israel since the twelfth century BC.'

'I thought we didn't believe in Christ.'

'Don't be smart. We believe he existed, we just don't buy the big PR push.'

'So why did we leave?'

'We didn't leave. We were driven out. First it was the Romans. Then in the seventh century along came the Persians. Then the Muslims. Then in the eleventh century it was the Christian Crusaders. Then in the sixteenth the Ottomans. And then in 1917 it was the British.'

So it was the British who'd given it to the UN to give to the Jews in 1948?

Dad scoffed and roared up like a tumour behind a driver doing fifty in the right-hand lane. 'No one gave it to us. We had to fight a war. Against the Arab League.'

'The Arab who?'

'The Arab League, sweetheart.' Mum, later that day, scrubbing the chip pan we'd left to soak. 'They opposed the creation of Israel by the UN and its recognition as a Jewish state. The day Israel announced statehood they invaded – forces from Egypt, Jordan, Lebanon and Syria. The Israeli army held them at bay and eventually they were able to take control of the area assigned to them in the Partition Plan.'

So the Arabs *were* there first?

Dad, the next week, laying a bin bag on the passenger seat before I could sit on it in my muddy kit: 'The British fucked it up for everyone. They promised the Arabs the land for an independent Arabic state in exchange for helping them defeat the Ottomans. *But* they promised it to the Jews too. And not just as an ad hoc stratagem, but because it was a moral imperative. And they wanted to dissuade too many of us from coming here.'

It was several more years before I bothered to brave the pre-Wiki internet to look up the Arab League or the Partition Plan (or what ottomans had to do with any of this), but this was the beginning of a new stage in my still-barely-existent relationship with Israel. Now, when it came up in prayers or in news reports, I felt a spasm of discomfort. It was pretty clear the British were the bad guys (as my dad had gone on to explain, they'd promised the land to the Jews before they'd even conquered it and without consulting the Muslims and Christians already living there), but still I felt uncomfortable at what I saw as Israel's complicity. It reminded me of when my sister Rachel was born and all of a sudden our house had shrunk by a third – although this analogy would work best, I later learned, if my parents had invited Rachels from around the world to move into my bedroom, and denied my right to return if I popped to the shops.

It would be stretching the truth quite far to say we had debates about this (my parents were too well informed and, unlike some people's parents who supported Israel with the cold, hard crust of the morally sure, too flexible, while I was still too ignorant, something I couldn't yet claim as a principle) but I definitely rolled my eyes any time a dinner guest mentioned a holiday in Eilat, or cleared my throat if they spoke about intifadas or the IDF. Resistance by snark attack. In a way, I realise now, I was exercising something central to my Jewish identity: sympathy with the underdog, caution of consensus. Or maybe I preferred to think of Jews as weak: the bespectacled nebbish, allergic to conflict, unwilling and unable to stand up for our interests.

But it was more complicated than that. How could it not be? In 2001, the year I went to Israel, there were forty bomb attacks launched against the Israeli populace within its borders and in the occupied territories. On my sixteenth birthday Hamas claimed responsibility for the bombing of a school bus in Nablus in the West Bank. Hamas, as I understood it, were a religiously extreme terrorist cult,[29] but they were also locked in a battle of legitimacy with the Ramallah government for control of Gaza and the West Bank, the two areas that Jewish settlers had occupied in contravention of the Fourth Geneva Convention of 1949 (which forbade countries from moving populations into territory occupied in war) and that Israel policed most heavy-handedly.[30] This battle for legitimacy didn't allow for the prospect of de-escalation or peaceful negotiations and relied on a climate (a cycle) of violence and retaliation, but this was a level of nuance I understood only later.

---

29 In fact, Hamas is a fascist theocracy whose founding charter calls, quite openly, for the murder of Jews: 'The Islamic Resistance Movement aspires to the realization of Allah's promise, no matter how long that should take: "The day of judgment will not come until Muslims kill the Jews. When the Jews will hide behind stones and trees, the stones and trees will say 'O Muslims, O Abdulla, there is a Jew behind me, come and kill him.'"' That Hamas hates Jews is one of the few parts of the Conflict not up for debate. Some suggested further reading: 'What Would Hamas Do If It Could Do Whatever It Wanted' by Jeffrey Goldberg in *The Atlantic*.

30 In June 2007 Hamas assumed control of Gaza.

The year after I went there were forty-seven bombs. One of those, a suicide attack, claimed thirty lives at a Passover Seder at the Park Hotel in the beach resort of Netanya. In response, at least ostensibly, Israel launched Operation Defensive Shield. Less poetically named than Operation Grapes of Wrath, which it had launched against Hezbollah a few years earlier in Lebanon, it was nevertheless the loudest military movement Israel had made into the West Bank since the 1967 Six Day War. It started with tanks rolling into Ramallah and placing Yasser Arafat under siege in his compound and continued with incursions into the five next-largest cities in the West Bank and their surrounding municipalities: Jenin, Nablus, Bethlehem, Tulkarm and Hebron.

This, unsurprisingly, led to fighting[31] and over the next few weeks, again in the run-up to my birthday, footage filtered through to living rooms around the nation. This was the sort of footage that made entrenched positions hard to maintain, particularly from the aerial bombardments of Jenin and Nablus. Here were images that cut to the quick: teenagers sprinting through dust-hued ruins, children huddled in front of shell-struck walls, wailing mothers who in their loss looked somehow biblical: what I'd always imagined from the phrase *gnashing their teeth*.

That year, with a suddenness in its onset that also seemed biblical, I'd suffered a bout of acne that had devastated my hitherto spot-free face. At first I'd ignored it, hoping it would leave with the suddenness it had arrived, but soon I could no longer do so. My skin was reptilian, my jawline crusted with purple pustules, and since doing nothing didn't seem to be doing much, I was forced to consider how to respond. The first response I favoured involved alternating hot and

31 According to UN estimates, 497 Palestinians were killed and another 1,447 injured, as well as/compared with thirty Israeli soldiers with 127 wounded.

cold flannels and a bottle of tea tree oil, which I applied directly to the spots morning and night, resisting the urge to squeeze, which, of course, would make it worse. For weeks I did this this religiously, which is to say, ritualistically and with no belief that it would work, and when it didn't I moved to the second option. Azelaic acid, which my GP had prescribed. This, as the name suggests, was the more hardcore solution (pun most definitely intended). It bleached my pillowcases and stained the collars of my school shirts the ugly yellow of a week-old bruise. You can imagine, then, what it did to my skin. It got rid of the acne, at least temporarily, but at some considerable dermatological cost. The skin around my mouth became silvery and so translucently thin it hurt to smile, which admittedly wasn't much of an issue, and in place of the spots I developed rashes that cracked into sores as painful as the spots were unsightly.

I say this not to be insensitive but because in the vortex of my teenage self-involvement the two issues (the Middle East and skincare) became somehow enmeshed. It seemed injudicious, not to mention disproportionate and cruel, to punish a region for the damage caused by a few individual insurgents, even if it was impossible to predict where the next one might erupt. Yes, these eruptions were devastating and just one could obliterate any sense of security a person or a nation might feel, but no good could come of such a unilateral response. If only from a tactical standpoint, such reactions radicalised more moderates than they neutralised radicals, and perpetuated the cycle of violence that Hamas (and Hezbollah) relied on to maintain viability. And that was before you considered the moral imperatives of a supposedly social democracy, one founded on the kibbutznik socialism of the early settlers. Watching the pictures of masses huddled against ruined infrastructure and crumbled architecture, I rubbed a hand against the rash on my jaw; and I'm ashamed to say that this was when Palestine started to seem personal.

Still, I didn't give it a lot more thought – not outside of my Friday night eye-rolls, not even at uni where I edited the paper and the Student Union had an official stance, which seemed to miscalculate its own importance – not until the summer of 2014. The summer of 2014, like the two previous, was spent in front of my laptop trying to write a follow-up to my first book, *Ostrich* (still available in some good bookshops, though it doesn't follow that if they don't stock it, they're not a good bookshop). I had an already approaching deadline and an idea I was bashing into shape: something about the grandson of a Holocaust survivor who starts to suspect his grandfather was really a camp guard rather than internee. The whole thing, though I didn't realise it then, was a study of his (my?) latent guilt at the fact he'd 'married out' and that his son, who would be born at the end (it wasn't then autobiographical) wouldn't be Jewish – and, later, a stealth attack on the false equivalence people love to draw between Jews and Nazis.[32] But back then it was just an interesting premise I thought I could stretch to a printable length, saved on my laptop as UntitledJewBook.doc.

I was on the lookout then for material that spoke to the Jewish experience, and I didn't have to look far to find it. The summer

---

32 This is a common analogy, often seen in the form of Israeli flags with a swastika in place of the Star of David, or even in literal mathematical expressions (one thing equalling the other). It's so obviously a wilful provocation that it does less to call attention to what it's ostensibly discussing (the treatment of the Palestinians) than it does to diminish a Jewish trauma that's still being felt. A bit like calling someone you're arguing with a cancer with the prior knowledge that their parents have died of cancer. The analogy's imperfect and simplistic (analogies always are; for one thing it conflates Israel and the Jews in a way many are guilty of doing) but it serves to illustrate the problem: there comes a point when insensitivity becomes something more deliberate.

of 2014 was dominated by two global events: the World Cup in Brazil, with its final contested between Germany and Argentina, and Israeli aggression in Gaza, the proximate cause for which was the kidnapping and murder by members of Hamas of three Israeli teenagers who were waiting for a bus in the West Bank. In response, as it tends to, Israel had sent forces into the region in search of the perpetrators, which prompted Hamas to launch rockets from Gaza into Israel.

The rest was grimly predictable, though even by the standards of one of the world's oldest conflicts the results were brutal. Israeli shelling seemed only to intensify, the images were even more disturbing than twelve years before, and by the operation's end around 2,200 Palestinians had been killed with estimates that around 65 per cent were unaffiliated with armed groups. This, then, was a summer of condemnation, of Facebook updates, TwitLongers and Medium posts, Avaaz emails and Change.org petitions, and, as usual, the pressure on Jews to speak out, either in defence or condemnation, was stronger than on most.

My Facebook feed was fairly evenly split while my Twitter timeline, which I curated more closely and better reflected my political outlook (left-wing, pessimistic), was united in damnation. Mostly I limited my participation to retweets and likes – I remember an article in the *Guardian* titled 'The World Stands Disgraced'. More than once I found my finger hovering above the publish button but ultimately I abstained: as I say, the one view I hold most assiduously is that Jews have no obligation to define themselves in relation to a foreign government's policy, and certainly not in a public forum to assuage strangers' discomfort. But as the summer wore on, and the images kept coming, I felt this conviction loosen. The moral obligation I had to speak out against what I was seeing didn't come from being Jewish, it came from being human. My Jewishness was

irrelevant and to pretend otherwise was narcissistic and disingenuous, an intellectual swerve that, since the discussion was only intellectual from afar, was also a moral failing.

I couldn't quite find the words to articulate these thoughts –
certainly not while staying true to my original credo – but when an
invite arrived in my notifications from Stop the War for a march to
Hyde Park, I was happy for the chance to talk with my feet – and
grateful to have something to post to Facebook that encompassed
my opposition succinctly and unequivocally.

On the day of the march I caught the Tube to Baker Street
and met a friend on the steps of All Souls Church on Langham
Place, just outside the giant glass molar of the BBC's Television
Centre, where the march was due to begin. I hadn't brought a
sign but we'd got there early and there were plenty of signs to
choose from: placards with slogans including END THE SIEGE,
STOP THE KILLING, END THE MASSACRE and STOP
THE GENOCIDE OF PALESTINIAN CHILDREN. I chose
an END THE SIEGE only to find it was double-sided and the
reverse said STOP THE GENOCIDE. There was a slight squirm
of uneasiness but I was able to suppress it. Now was not the time
for semantics, something I have a natural proclivity for. In times
of moral certitude hyperbole was justified, maybe even morally
required.

Likewise I didn't have a problem with the numerous homemade signs that likened Israel to a terrorist state or a fascist regime,
or even (generously) with the sign held by a boy of maybe ten that
featured that most broken equation: Jews equalled Nazis. The key
was the context, and the context was that people were dying – actually dying – by consequence of the actions of a government who'd
been democratically elected, and so were subject to the vicissitudes

of public opinion.[33] Whether or not their deaths constituted a genocide was not the most important consideration, it was that they were ongoing and avoidable.

Odd, then, that the one thing I should take umbrage with, the one thing that caused a discomfort I couldn't shake, was the proud announcement by one of the protest's organisers that the march contained a special Jewish section. At the time I wasn't sure quite why this made me so uncomfortable besides the obvious fact that the Jews had been marked out, segregated in a march for human rights, but looking back I can characterise it thus: I'd explicitly put my Jewishness aside to be here, I'd overcome a fear of crowds that I don't think is unrelated, and now I was being told that my Jewishness was a coveted currency. The implication – that I wasn't just here as a person, that my voice had an extra resonance – was a responsibility I hadn't asked for and precisely the reason I'd resisted weighing in online.[34]

Also there was the knowledge of why the organisers would be so proud of this. Were there people in that crowd of thousands who harboured anti-Semitic views? Almost – and I'm being very careful – certainly. And was there a small minority whose anti-Zionism was a cover for an older, less socially progressive hatred? Again, this was highly possible, and a conversation that needed to be had at some later date, when the shelling had stopped. But this announcement seemed to be cutting

33 By this rationale I even understand why people march more against Israel than other countries with equally bad or much worse human rights records, e.g. China or Saudi Arabia. Because it feels like there's a chance, albeit slim, that someone might listen.

34 Maybe you do think Jews have an extra responsibility to speak out against Israel. Maybe you also believe Israel is a terrorist state. If you do, I bet you don't also believe that Muslims need to speak out against Islamist terror attacks and that if they don't they invite Islamophobia.

off this discussion at the turn. It was a pre-emptive defence against accusations that hadn't yet been made. The message, if unintended, was clear: the presence of Jews made the march above board. Without us, it was vulnerable to all kinds of innuendo, but with us it was kosher. The Jews, made separate from the rest of the crowd, were its insurance.

◆ ◆ ◆

In 2018 I wrote a piece for the *Independent*. It wasn't about Israel. In fact, it was mostly about how all discussions of Jewish experience at one point or another are dragged round to Israel, and the comments beneath, as usual, did much to support this observation. Many – a vast majority – of the commenters assumed, although I'd been critical of Israel, that I was a closet Zionist, and that in pointing out this rhetorical sinkhole (in which those pointing out anti-Semitism are assumed to have a Zionist agenda) I was seeking to subvert the debate and silence legitimate criticism. I was called a Zio and Zionazi, accused of writing (under a different name) for a far-right website, of being a member of an Islamophobic think tank, and attempting to smear a leading politician the piece only glancingly mentioned.

But the most stringent criticism came via email from a member of my family. In it they registered their upset that I had been dismissive and critical of Israel and suggested it was unhelpful, even dangerous, if Jews failed to show a united front; that in claiming I had no affiliation with Israel I had inadvertently suggested the link was tenuous for every Jew. This family member went on to enumerate various points I hadn't covered (again, the article was not about Israel). Did I know that Palestinian Arab Israelis had equal rights to Jewish Israelis, that it was an Arab Israeli judge who sentenced Olmert, a former prime minister, to jail? Or that Ariel Sharon had withdrawn from Gaza in the hope of achieving peace only for an Iranian proxy to set up shop?

I didn't know these things and wasn't sure if they were true. Neither could I speak to the veracity of many of the claims made in the comments: that Israel monitored the calories going into Gaza to ensure the populace was kept undernourished; that it had illegally incarcerated hundreds of thousands of Palestinian citizens since 1967. It's possible that all these points are true to a greater or lesser extent – certainly none would appear to disprove another – and it's certainly true that each side believes they have the moral right to present the facts in certain lights, but really I'm the last person who'd know. It could be that my ignorance is unusual, that I've cultivated it for too long to gain back the ground, or it could be it's reflective of a more general condition. Not every Jew is an expert in Middle Eastern politics. Nor do we need to be.

But I do feel qualified to talk about what Israel means as a symbol, what its existence confers and why (while it's extremely dangerous to conflate Jewishness with a political stance) I think a majority of British Jews do support the idea of the Jewish state.[35] One thing my family member wrote did stay with me, although I can't say I agree with it: 'Israel provides every Jew with an essential cloak of security. Having this security enables us to voice our views, to display our heritage, to hold our heads high . . . The existence of Israel gives you the strength, consciously or unconsciously, to express your views in print.'

So here we are again at fences round cultural centres and tyre irons in the glove compartment. Perhaps there is some truth to

---

35 Which is not the same as condoning illegal settlements or support-ing the actions of a far-right, ethno-nationalist government; I abhor our current government with every fibre in my being but at no point in the past nine years have I questioned Britain's right to exist.

the idea that the world is more comfortable with Jews when we embrace our weakness than celebrate our strength, but to divorce Israel from that *cloak of security* is a dangerous game. Whether you believe a Jewish state is necessary – and to a lesser extent whether you believe it's justified in defending (and, to an even lesser extent, expanding) its borders – depends, I suppose, largely on whether you feel Jews in Europe and elsewhere require such a cloak, whether we've fully integrated (or been allowed to fully integrate) into our host societies, and whether there's a possibility, however slight, that our hosts might ever reject us. Personally I still find the idea that Israel would ever be a safer place for me to live than where I currently do almost impossible to imagine, but that's not to say I don't believe in its existence. The question it was founded on was a lot less hypothetical. Israel exists because the Holocaust happened, not because it might happen again; once was enough.

At a point in history when two thirds of Europe's Jewry had been exterminated, with their murderers uncharged, it seems reasonable to me that the world needed a Jewish state. None of this is to condone the tragedy of Palestinian displacement nor the illegality and, to my mind, immorality of the settlements, nor to minimise or excuse any of the subsequent tragedies visited upon the Palestinian people who have suffered worst from a cycle of violence that does as much to advance the careers of right-wing ideologues as it does to legitimise Hamas, but it's important to remember that Israel exists, primarily, because it *needed* to. Know that every Jew you meet has a member of their family who was forced to leave their homeland because it was hostile to Jews. Anti-Semitism created Israel, and not, as some would have it, the other way around.

This is not to say I'm comfortable calling myself a Zionist, even by the definition that most Jews would agree on (a believer in the need for a Jewish state), and despite everything I've said and can intellectually support I *do* think Jews have a moral duty to speak out against crimes that at least in the abstract are committed in our name – *dayenu*.

But this belief is secondary – and firmly so – to the belief that every Jew is entitled to their opinion and to the choice of whether they share it. No one is entitled to a stranger's views on a subject so loaded with connotations, and anyone who stipulates a Jew denounce Israel or adopt their definition of Zionism before entering a conversation can go bang their head on a wall. This applies, too, to anyone who leverages someone's Jewishness as a way to amplify their criticism of Israel or uses it as an excuse to ignore other Jewish voices, and it applies doubly to those who respond to stories about domestic Jewish experience by demanding that we first talk about Palestine. (And maybe – uncomfortable as it is for me to consider – there's some truth in what my family member wrote to me: that it's partly because of Israel that I can say this.)

Chapter Six:
Race

In December 2016, in the wake of Donald Trump's election to the White House, *The Atlantic* published an article written by the journalist Emma Green, with the provocative title 'Are Jews White?', with the aim of answering a question that has plagued Jews and racists for almost as long as the correct pronunciation of 'bagel', and whether white hoods with all-white robes is a touch on the nose: are Jews a race?

The context for the piece, which was shared widely on social media, was the closing ads then-candidate Trump had run as part of his successful presidential campaign. These ads, Trump's *Argument for America*, were well produced, incisively written, powerfully delivered and ultimately effective, and featured a series of anti-Semitic dog whistles from which the word 'dog' could probably be omitted. Over blanched-out footage of the prominent Jewish financier and philanthropist George Soros – a long-time bogeyman for the Republican right who has been variously accused of fixing elections and funding anti-Trump protests, a man who at fourteen saw his native Hungary overrun by the Nazis – the soon-to-be commander-in-chief's narration warned that '[t]he establishment has trillions of dollars at stake in this election, for those who control the levers of power in Washington and for global special interests.' The footage of Soros played until the *for* before *global special interests*, at which point it gave way to footage of Janet Yellen, the Jewish former head of the Federal Reserve. Later in the video, which played in the final week before the election, footage of the Jewish Goldman Sachs CEO Lloyd Blankfein was introduced thus: 'It's a global power structure that have [*sic*] robbed our working class, stripped our country of its wealth and put that money into the pockets of a handful of large corporations and political entities.' Earlier in the campaign, attempting to tie his opponent Hillary Clinton to Goldman Sachs, Trump had tweeted an image of her under the hashtag 'America First' in which she was superimposed over a sea of dollars next to copy labelling her *[the] Most Corrupt Candidate Ever!* This copy was contained inside a six-pointed star. In an amended image, posted two hours later, the star had been replaced by a circle.

The article was also concerned with Trump's choice for chief strategist, Steve Bannon, ex-TV producer[36] and founder of the Breitbart News Network, a right-wing alt-news hell mouth that promoted white supremacists and frequently peddled in anti-Semitic language and conspiracy.[37] Despite these alarming signs, many in the States, Jewish and otherwise, dismissed concerns that Jews had anything to fear from a Trump presidency. In mitigation

---

36 Alleged to have made $32 million from the syndication of the 'too Jewish' *Seinfeld*.

37 It's Breitbart, and specifically Bannon, that is credited with the popularisation of *globalist* as an anti-Semitic dog whistle, as in 'Globalists Unite: Clinton Running Mate Dines with George Soros' Son'; 'Orbán: Globalists Will Use Mass Migration to Replace Europeans and "Crush the Will of the People"'. But they're not always so subtle: 'Planned Parenthood Body Count is up to Half a Holocaust'; 'Bill Kristol: Republican Spoiler, Renegade Jew' – both headlines from the year of Trump's election.

for his dabbling in anti-Semitic tropes and his hiring of a chief strategist who allegedly was uncomfortable with his daughters attending school with Jews,[38] they cited the wildly capricious, historically illiterate narcissist's support of Israel, his apparent fondness for Benjamin Netanyahu (who appeared to fit the 'strong man' type he favoured in world leaders), and the fact that the daughter he most wanted to sleep with had converted to Judaism.

But the article acknowledged that not all Jews felt so secure. For some, Trump's election had reminded them of their otherness, that they occupied a familiar historical position: 'set apart' through their Jewishness 'and thus left vulnerable'. And it was to its titular question that it repeatedly returned. Quoting Eric Goldstein, an associate professor of History at Emory University: 'Jewish identity in America is inherently paradoxical and contradictory. What you have is a group that was historically considered, and considered itself, an outsider group, a persecuted minority. In the space of two generations, they've become one of the most successful, integrated groups in American society – by many accounts, part of the establishment. And there's a lot of dissonance between those two positions.'

Or as the journalist herself explained, Jews as a category remain problematic, their status ambiguous in spite (or because) of what prestige they amass. If 'white' is a marker denoting power then (some) Jews must be said to be white, 'but they are also often viewed with suspicion'. Ultimately, the piece concludes, the titular question is a misnomer that when examined gives way to the real one beneath it: 'Are Jews White?' means are 'Are Jews safe?' To many the answer to this question is obvious: obviously so and obviously not.

---

38 In 2007, Bannon's ex-wife signed a court document alleging he hadn't wanted their daughters to attend Archer, a Los Angeles high school, because of 'the number of Jews that attend'.

Predictably, the piece, which is excellent, drew criticism from several quarters, not least from those who hadn't read beyond the headline. Some of the criticism, again predictably, came from the right, who'd likely arrived at it through Google searches and who rejected the premise that Trump or Bannon had said anything that warranted an article being written; but as much, if not more, came from the left, *The Atlantic*'s core readership, who disputed the idea that Jews were in the firing line when other targets of Trump's rhetoric had been left in no doubt of their status as unwanted. This argument was taking place across an ocean for which the publication that was hosting it was named and in a new age of truth-phobic nativism that had no precedent in my living memory, but it reminded me powerfully of another election, specifically an incident that had also taken place in the last leg of the run-up to the polls.

In 2015, before Brexit, Corbyn, backstops and constitutional crises, the Labour party was led by the less photogenic but more politically adept of two brothers from Fitzrovia. Ed Miliband had been seen by most as an unlikely winner in a leadership contest that had been billed by many as a feud between brothers with near-biblical overtones, but had emerged as a plausible alternative to the Cameron-fronted Tory–Lib Dem coalition that had been muddling through its programme of public-facing soft social progressivism and backdoor fiscal conservatism since its rushed inception in 2010. He'd impressed on the campaign trail with pledges to protect the NHS and cut tuition fees and (it's worth noting) a manifesto that doubled down on Tory rhetoric (and policy) on immigration, and was neck-and-neck with Cameron in the polls.

Since the sitting PM had refused to debate him, the first major televisual event of the election was to happen on 26 March: both candidates would be interviewed by the nation's premier political hitman, *Newsnight*'s Jeremy Paxman. The incumbent David

Cameron, running on the trifecta of strong leadership, a clear economic plan and a brighter, more secure future with the additional promise of a referendum on the country's EU membership to satisfy a regressive fringe of his party, went first. Unlike much of the electorate he appeared undiminished from five years of Tory rule, but ten minutes under studio lighting seemed to age him ten years. All but the most decided would conclude that his mauling had been thorough, that he'd withered under what Malcolm Tucker once memorably referred to as the host's 'horse face of mock incredulity'. (Could he live on a zero-hour contract? The answer never came. I guess we'll never know.) And then it was Miliband.

In the opening forays he acquitted himself surprisingly well – most of us feared the worst. He was at ease with the crowd during the audience Q&A that preceded the interview, far more than Cameron had been, straying from his talking points and engaging in what could almost be termed repartee. He spoke candidly(ish) about the rift with his brother, and early in the seated interview appeared to have defanged Paxman with the simple but seldom-seen tactic of fronting up to a mistake.[39] As the interview progressed things seemed to get better. Paxman did as Paxman does, hammering away at a single question like a pre-noughties chatbot attempting to pass the Turing test, but Miliband's responses, while evasive, played less like Cameron's evasions and more like a desire to elevate the debate over pure numbers. Eventually, as far as is possible in a cage with a well-prepped lion, he seemed to start to relax. On falling living standards and the drop in real wages he was informed and impassioned, and entering the final rounds it was Paxman who appeared on the back

39 On the Labour party's history of failing to meet its own targets for immigration: 'We got it wrong. We got it wrong.' It is worth noting that 2015 Labour's commitment to immigration targets and its party line about low-skilled migrants undercutting the minimum wage has been lost in Miliband's subsequent teddybearification.

foot. The eyebrow remained hooked, the posture relaxed, like he was reclining in an armchair at the Groucho, but it belied the fact that he was struggling for traction, muddling his words (*exempt* for *exert*), reaching to land a significant blow.

And then he did. Miliband had just landed a glove of his own, drawing applause from the audience for accusing Paxman of presuming to decide the election six weeks before the polls opened ('You're important, Jeremy, but you're not that important'),[40] and had defended himself impressively from accusations that he was a liability on the doorsteps: 'The papers can write what they want, the man on the Tube can say what he wants. All I care about is the British people . . . I know this country can be so much better.' But the interviewer had a look on his face, the brow stretched to its elastic limit, like he knew the next words from his mouth would be tomorrow morning's headlines. He uncrossed his arms and spoke over the applause.

'The thing is . . . they [the public] see you as a North London geek.'

Watching at home I felt something cold at the base of my spine. It was jarring at once – it seemed cruel, needlessly personal, far more so than anything Cameron had had to endure – but at first I couldn't say precisely why I'd had such a physical response. Was I offended as a geek? In part. But that didn't explain the discomfort looping from my brain to my gut and back. It was partly also the relish with which he'd said it, but pretty quickly I knew that wasn't it either. It wasn't the *geek* part but what had directly preceded it. What the hell *was* a 'North London geek'? I'd lived in North London all my life and had

---

40 'Hell yeah, I'm tough enough' also, it's worth noting, drew applause from the studio that night and only later in its memefication became a punchline.

never encountered the concept. And why would I? Geekdom was not (is not) geographically bounded. Nor were geeks disproportionately concentrated in particular areas; as far as I knew they were distributed evenly throughout the population, a staple of every teen drama and coming-of-age story ever written, regardless of setting. Besides which, by my own definition Miliband wasn't even from North London. Fitzrovia was Zone One, and so exempt from the North–South animosities.

And then there was the way Miliband, the son of Polish and Belgian immigrants, had been portrayed throughout the campaign. There was the *Daily Mail* 'exposé' on his father, Ralph, a famed Marxist intellectual, under the headline 'The Man Who Hated Britain', and then there was the infamous picture, the subject of a *Sun* front page a year after its taking and subject to sustained commentary, of him eating a sandwich.[41] The implication, as with much of the coverage of Miliband – his awkward gait, his nasal voice – was that this man was unlike us. He was a stranger in our midst, an alien, somehow – indefinably but obviously – *other*.[42]

'Did he just call him a Jew?' asked Imogen, who was sitting beside me.

As it turned out, Paxman was right to be sceptical of Labour's ability to win a majority, or even to prevent the Tories from doing so. There may have been nothing between them in the polls at the time of the interviews but Cameron went on to win at a canter and the rest, as they say, is history, albeit the type future students will pray doesn't come up in the test. To be clear: I'm

41 I defy you to find one caption that doesn't mention the filling. The *Sun*'s headline features three separate puns on it: 'Save Our Bacon', 'Pig's Ear' and 'Don't Swallow his Porkies'.

42 For more on this, quaint though it now seems, read Boyd Tonkin in the *Independent*: 'Is criticism of Ed Miliband a coded form of anti-Semitism?'

not suggesting Paxman's 'geek' was a decisive factor in handing Cameron the election, nor that this was the *Sliding Doors* of recent British politics, where the timelines forked and in the other we're enjoying a decade of progress and prosperity (that, I think, was when Gordon Brown was forced to apologise for calling a bigot a bigot). Neither am I accusing Jeremy Paxman of knowingly blowing an anti-Semitic dog whistle; far more likely it was unconscious, although he appeared to know the damage it would cause. But nevertheless, in three short words, perforated with an almost-deniable pause, he succeeded in articulating a discomfort the British electorate evidently felt for a candidate that had little to do with his politics – and, I'd argue, a discomfort with a culture at large. Something about Miliband's face didn't fit. And in Britain, in 2015 and again in 2020, your face not fitting is a euphemism for something that requires more thought.

Whether or not Jews are white is a question that needs unpicking and restitching before it can be answered, one that rests on a series of suppositions about race, whiteness, acceptance and oppression – not to mention intersections of wealth and class – that we rarely think of in debates about prejudice. Ultimately, it's not a question that needs answering but nevertheless is instructive of the awkward status that Jews enjoy/endure in a society whose dominant culture, and the lens through which it understands itself, is still white.

On a personal level it's a question I'm forced to consider with each council funding consultation or each time I take my son to a new playgroup. No box seems accurately to capture my experience or my feelings towards it. Am I White British? Ostensibly, yes – and when it comes to race (and racism) it's the ostensibly that should matter. But then why does the sight of a flag, even in the context of a World Cup, make me want to cross the road to avoid it? Depending on my mood I'll swallow my pride and just tick the box or, if it's an option, opt for White Other. But only if there's no requirement to specify the otherness. If Jewish were a box I'd tick it without thought, but to add it by hand seems a contrivance too far. And there's rarely the space for eight thousand words.

What, then, is race? What is whiteness? If it's the privilege of not considering your racial identity even when confronted with a spectrum of alternatives, like those people who don't think they're political or think they don't have an accent, then I grew up white. If it's seeing yourself reflected as a default in a culture that robs minorities of representation and only permits them to define themselves through their deviation from a baseline you set, then I'm white too. If it's the knowledge that your institutions are here to serve you, the opportunities to achieve a status partially predetermined by the colour of your skin, and the likelihood of being born into wealth, then I'm three for three, or five for five. But if it's the security – both felt and actual – that comes with the above, the confidence that comes from expecting to be judged by the content of your character, and the presumption that your identity won't be held meaningfully against you, that you won't be attacked for it, well, then I'm no longer so sure. Culturally, I don't identify as white, but then who besides racists would?

White culture is a misunderstanding in the same way the British Museum is the world's most brazen crime scene,[43] but that's not to deny there are experiences that are common to white people, ostensible or otherwise. Gone if not forgotten are the days when Jews were banned from clubs and institutions on the back of their

---

43 Despite what *Back to the Future* posits it wasn't really Marty McFly, via Chuck Berry's cousin, who invented rock 'n' roll.

Jewishness[44] and like most (but not all) Jews, I benefit from white privilege in ways too many to enumerate and probably in ways I haven't even noticed. Chiefly there are few spaces, physical or virtual, I feel excluded from and few if any opportunities that have been denied me on the basis of my skin. In this regard, I have not lived as a racial minority and should have no qualms about owning my whiteness, construct though it is, since I've only benefitted from it. My hesitation is a form of vanity, a wish to distance myself from an imperialist past and a present built on discrimination and historical exploitation that hasn't begun to 'even out'.

In her essential 2017 book *Why I'm No Longer Talking to White People About Race*, the journalist Reni Eddo-Lodge makes the case that race and class should be considered in tandem, as dual forces, distinct but interrelated, that can jointly determine the opportunities a person is afforded. Class, she argues, is less about self-perception (according to the 2016 British Social Attitudes survey, 47 per cent of those who considered themselves working class were in managerial or professional jobs) than about the material reality. In this material reality, members of BAME communities are far likelier to experience income poverty as an adult, to live in poverty as a child, to be unemployed or to work in low-skilled jobs.[45] As Eddo-Lodge herself explains, the evidence suggests that privileging race over class or class over race when considering the structural inequalities our society is

---

44 Editing this book I learned that in 1954 the Globe Tennis Club in Belsize Park was founded because the club in neighbouring West Hampstead didn't admit Jews. In the mid-1960s Woody Allen was best known as a stand-up and for a shaggy dog routine about a Jewish couple who attend a fancy-dress party dressed as a moose, only for the husband to be shot, decapitated, mounted and hung in the New York Athletic Club. The joke is on them because it's restricted.

45 According to data from the Joseph Rowntree Foundation (2007) and the 2011 British census, both cited in *Why I'm No Longer Talking to White People About Race*.

built on is neither easy nor advisable.[46] Which brings us to the tricky subject of Jews and money.

The perception, certainly among anti-Semites but probably in the population at large, is that Jews have lots of it. The reality, of course, is that there are rich Jews and poor Jews and the rich ones are more visible (what Jewish psychologist Daniel Kahneman would call an availability bias), but it is true that Jewish people are overrepresented in some high-paying professions. In some cases the explanation is simple and stems directly from historical oppression. Jews are well represented in the commercial art world, for example, because for much of the twentieth century our bank accounts were subject to seizure. Similarly Jewish people have historically numbered highly in business and finance because we were excluded from professional guilds and forbidden from owning land, which forced us into work as merchants and bookkeepers. But in some cases, the relation between the field and the numbers is more complicated and open to varied explanations.

Take Jews in law, for example, of which there are proportionally high numbers. Is this the result of parental pressure to achieve academically and professionally (a stereotype that has some basis in fact); Talmudic study with its focus on textual analysis and the transferable skills it fosters; some cultural emphasis on argumentation; the prohibitions on land ownership; the fact that Jews are a small community and so more likely to personally know someone in the field already; or some combination of the above? Or is it something more sinister, a serendipitous alignment of negative stereotypes? People don't trust lawyers and people don't trust Jews. Ergo, Jews must make the best lawyers.

---

46 It's no coincidence that when black celebrities achieve a certain level of fame and wealth they're often said to have 'transcended race'.

In *Curb Your Enthusiasm*, the sitcom created by Larry David (who started his career as a traditional nebbish of the Allen school but has since evolved into something more interesting), one memorable plot has Larry appalled to discover that his divorce lawyer, Berg, is not Jewish but Swedish. What's more, Berg has fostered the misunderstanding, displaying a *shofar* on his desk and dropping crumbs of Hebrew and Yiddish. The joke relies on the presumption that Jews are not just well represented in the field of law as a matter of coincidence, but that their Jewishness equips them for its scheming and dealings. Why else would Larry be so distressed? 'She's gonna get *everything*!' (Similarly, when displaced socialite Alexis Rose is required to impersonate a lawyer to intimidate an adversary in a 2016 episode of the Canadian sitcom *Schitt's Creek* she instinctively identifies herself as Angelica Bloomfield of the fictional law firm Rose, Bloomfield and Glickman.)

Certainly though, it's true that the correlation between ethnicity and social status doesn't appear to hold in the case of Jews. And if racism isn't structural – enforced by institutions, by unconscious bias, by the diminishment of its victims' life chances – is it really racism? Those who complain about anti-white racism make a good (unwitting) case that it's not. If racism is prejudice plus the power to enforce it, it's difficult to argue that anti-Semitism functions the same way as anti-black or anti-Asian racism, that Jews aren't part of the white establishment. And then there's the issue of visibility – the fact you'd have to argue it at all. Race, like class, is a construct, but it's one that generally resists self-perception. You can identify white people because they're white. In all but exceptional cases, my Jewishness is something I can choose to disclose, which brings an element of self-determination denied the victim of more traditional racial prejudice because I can control if and when to 'out' myself as Jewish and, therefore, the effect my

Jewishness has over a given situation.[47] So in a situation where it might be detrimental I can choose to withhold it – as all Jewish kids are routinely taught to do. By contrast, this is not a privilege afforded other ethnic minorities.

The recent Bias in Britain poll conducted by the *Guardian* found that 38 per cent of the thousand BAME participants surveyed had been falsely suspected of shoplifting in the past five years (compared to 14 per cent of white people). Forty-three per cent felt they'd been overlooked for a job or a promotion in a way that seemed unfair (more than twice the percentage for Caucasians), while 12 per cent had been the target of racist language in the last year, rising to 43 per cent over five years. Muslim men were the most likely to have been stopped by the police, while Muslim women were 'more likely to have felt the need to alter their appearance because of their ethnicity'.[48]

Perhaps, then, if my Jewishness were more visible, less deniable – if I wore a kippah, say, or had *payot*[49] – my experience would be closer to that of BAME communities and I'd have an easier time seeing myself as non-white. But if I did wear a kippah or have payot I'd be a different type of Jew and, statistically speaking, much more likely to view my Jewishness as a religious identity (as opposed to an ethnic one),[50] and, by extension, view anti-Semitism as anti-religious.

---

47 There is a major exception to this rule which is discussed in the next chapter.

48 Afua Hirsch, writing in the *Guardian*.

49 The tightly coiled waterslide sideburns worn by Orthodox Jews, whose experience is a long way from my own.

50 If you think about it, it makes sense that non-religious Jews are more likely to view their Jewishness as an ethnicity since, if it's not a religion, what is it?

But this too seems absurd. To suggest that the hatred endured by Jews for the past few millennia is a hatred of our customs, our practice, is a blindness as wilful as the demagogue who denies white privilege or the liberal who doesn't see colour. Clearly if Jews aren't a race they've been racialised by centuries of being singled out, massacred, expelled, displaced. It's obvious anti-Semites have little squeamishness in seeing Jews as a race (often another species), and defining a group in reductive terms they haven't agreed on is another definition of racism.

And there is more than one type of racism. It's true that Jews as a group aren't subject to the same disadvantages as some other minorities, that as white-passing we enjoy certain privileges, but the deniability of Jewishness is linked directly to how anti-Semitism works, and to its own deniability. Anti-Jewish racism, at least at this point in human history, is not concerned with maintaining an underclass by failing to meaningfully address historic inequalities – preserving hierarchies and ensuring the scales don't tip – but is a form of insurance. If Jews are successful and seen to be thriving in a system that suits their needs, they can serve as the scapegoat when the system stops working. Unlike traditional racism, which tends to be binary, relying on a few baseless stereotypes, anti-Jewish racism is quantum: Jews are at once weak beyond pity and powerful beyond belief.

We see this in the fervently held conspiracies that Jews are behind every disaster of the twenty-first century: 9/11, the Iraq War, the financial crash, even weather fronts and natural disasters. 'Jews will not replace us,' chanted the white supremacists marching through Charlottesville (the ones 'the least racist man you could ever meet' called 'very fine people'), not because they feared we'd replace them demographically (how could we?) but because Jews were orchestrating a global campaign to weaken America's borders and funding caravans of dangerous illegal immigrants.[51]

All of this relies on the perception (and partial reality) that Jews are successful, clever, that we're on the inside pissing out. If Jews were coded as poor, as just weak as opposed to also almighty, would Hitler have been able to unite a fractured Germany in the belief that we were behind all their troubles? Would parties around Europe, like Jobbik and Golden Dawn, make such gains promising to stand up to us?

And there is another unique aspect to anti-Semitism, another way in which it differs from other racism: its cross-party appeal. It's not just the white nationalists on the far right that have a problem with Jews; many on the left have fallen short of standing up to anti-Semitism, and in many cases peddle the same tropes and conspiracy theories invented by their political counterparts. That Jews are white grants us certain advantages and rights, like the privilege of shopping without a security guard lurking over our shoulder, but it also denies us the protection of a united left, who are uncomfortable with the notion of white victimhood – and are equally susceptible to talk of global elites and supranational motives. Ironically, it may be that Jews are unwelcome on the right because we're not white enough and unwelcome on the left for the opposite reason, because we're too white, because we fail to fit some victim archetype, as if through the result of some bizarre reverse profiling. How else to explain the scepticism (often hostility) with which those reporting anti-Semitism on the left are routinely met? Either our

---

51 Certainly this was the belief of Robert Bowers, who on 27 October 2018 walked into the Tree of Life synagogue in Pittsburgh and opened fire with an automatic weapon, killing eleven Jews. Minutes before the attack he'd posted the following to social media site Gab in reference to this belief: 'I can't sit by and watch my people get slaughtered. Screw your optics, I'm going in.'

motives will be questioned, itself an anti-Semitic trope, or we're accused of hysteria, or of misreading intent, as if being punched in the head doesn't hurt if the person was aiming at someone standing over your shoulder.[52]

And if they are accepted, the specificity of our concerns is diluted. This, for example, is what happened when the secretary of a local Labour branch in County Durham, Steve Cooke, tabled an emergency motion condemning the fatal attack in Pittsburgh: '[Colleagues] said that all the focus was on "antisemitism this, anti-semitism that", while other types of racism never even got a mention . . . They wanted references to antisemitism removed from the Pittsburgh motion . . . [NAME REDACTED] said that the person alleged to be responsible for the Pittsburgh murders was a far-right activist, a Nazi, which was the very opposite of what the Labour Party stood for. Yes, I responded, that's why the motion condemns what he did, describes his long-held antisemitic views and states the party's opposition to such bigotry. I said that I would be happy to add "far-right, neo-Nazi activities" to the motion's clause noting that "the alleged perpetrator of this heinous act is reported to have had a long history of antisemitic views and held a deep hatred for Jewish people", but the comrades weren't prepared to accept that proposal either.' Later, Steve was 'accused of trying to bring the party into disrepute by associating [it] with antisemitism'.

And herein lies the issue. Without wishing to equate the threat posed by a far-right terrorist and a local chapter of a left-wing

---

52 In many senses our current culture war can be understood in terms of intent and effect. Broadly speaking the right believes in the sanctity of the former, in racist bones and their absence in people's bodies, while the left (rightly, I think) measures an offence by the effect on its victims. When it comes to anti-Semitism, though, this supposition is revoked; all that matters is whether the speaker *intended* any harm.

parliamentary party – one is obviously greater than the other – Jews are either 'white' or not, in a way that never entirely seems to serve our best interests. Our whiteness can be revoked or reinforced simultaneously and according to whose agenda it suits at a particular moment. The murder of eleven Jews in a synagogue is not enough to permit the suggestion that Jews might have been a specific target – and that Jew hatred might have a particular, irreducible nature. By denying this specificity some on the left, intentionally or otherwise, deny the specificity of Jewish experience; even racism against us is whitewashed, the progressive equivalent of All Lives Matter.

If Jews can't be acknowledged as victims of racial prejudice even in the direct aftermath of a terror attack in a shul, then what hope can we have that political movements of any persuasion are capable of grasping the nuances of our position or willing to consider the multivalence of our existence?

Ultimately, the question 'Are Jews White?' speaks to a discomfort that goes in two directions. As a Jew I'm not fully comfortable around those who consider me a Jew first and Caucasian second, but neither am I at ease with those who consider me white with no asterisk, without a wider discussion of what that whiteness connotes. I suppose this means, by my own reckoning, that I'm caught between stalls, a helpless contrarian, resistant to labels, claiming special circumstances while pleading for equal treatment, but the line I keep returning to is Alvy Singer's 'key joke', a line most often attributed to Groucho Marx but one that, as Alvy knows, first appears in Freud's *Wit and its Relation to the Unconscious*: 'I'd never want to belong to any club that would have someone like me as a member.' Does the corollary hold? As a Jew, lapsed or otherwise, is it logical that I should wish to belong to a club that wouldn't have someone like me in its ranks?

So are Jews white? Some questions don't need answering since just the fact that they're asked is answer enough. Are you famous? Did you cum? But some questions needn't be asked because deciding on an answer achieves so little. When it comes to anti-racism you don't have to pick a squad of eligible minorities whose victimisation you're prepared to stand up against. Nor, despite what the current state of our political discourse would seem to suggest, is anti-racism a zero-sum game; you don't oppose anti-Semitism at the expense of decrying Islamophobia, or vice versa. (As the meme goes, find you a man who can do both.) There are no league tables for racism, no requirement to pick a side beyond racist or not, and it's all of our moral duties to listen to minorities and understand their concerns, no matter their origins, or how oppressed we perceive them to be.

It would be overstating the point to say I think about this stuff each time I'm presented with a form to fill in, that my pen hovers over the box like a circling passenger jet awaiting approval from air traffic control, but only slightly. For me, as I suspect for many Jewish people, an awareness of the contradictions that lie at the heart of my Jewishness is never far from the surface but, when push comes to shove, as it inevitably does, and as with all matters concerning race, the choice is not ours to make; it will be made by racists, on internet message boards, in parliamentary debates, on Twitter or Fox News, in the White House, in online manifestos and marching through universities with flaming torches held aloft. For now, then, let's say this: most Jews are white, but only when it suits others, and right up to the point that we're not. And it's this precarity that best encapsulates the Jewish experience of race.

Chapter Seven:
The Internet

I still remember my first email address and the excitement of getting it. This was the summer of my trip to Israel, and to solidify new friendships and consolidate failed romances I would need to get an account on MSN Messenger, which required I have an email address from Hotmail.com. The address I chose, of the literally infinite available, was a homage to the comedian Mark Lamarr and his appearances on the anarchic cult TV quiz show *Shooting Stars*, a show I'd seen just a handful of episodes of. Armed with my mg_1950sconman handle (a conflation of two references I'd only half-heard: '1950s scamp' and 'cheeky cockney conman'),[53] I entered a shadow world of late-night confessions and text-based flirtation.

In those days, when connecting to it required a dormant phone line and a tolerance for free-form techno, before anyone had heard of echo chambers or algorithms, the internet was a curious, top-loading playground with a kitschy, kooky homemade aesthetic. It was democratic in a way little else was. The old media stalwarts, yet to discover a model to monetise the

---

53 To make matters worse, people thought I just really liked scones.

content they were mostly giving away for free, competed with amateurs, cranks and hobbyists in the new attention economy. This was years before Twitter and Facebook would further flatten the field with publishing templates that lent everyone, from Pulitzer prize-winners to bedroom contrarians, the same level of legitimacy. But even so, anyone with a keyboard and basic HTML could produce 'news' that looked much the same as stories coming from reputable sources in professional news rooms. The aesthetic hierarchy, maintained by the exorbitant costs of printing and distributing news, had collapsed, ushering in a new era of increased credulity and blanket distrust. Ultimately it was the rise of the internet that would facilitate (and accelerate) our path towards where we are today, in our separate bubbles,[54] surrounded by those who uphold our worldview, at war with the concept of objective truth.

But back in 2001 none of this seemed cause for alarm, at least not outside Fleet Street, since the separation between life at the keyboard and life away from it could hardly have been wider. I started my first relationship on MSN and when we met in person what intimacy we'd achieved was jarringly absent. We broke up on MSN too and I called her later that evening to do it again. One popular trick, I remember, was to confess a crush to someone online. If the window fell silent, you simply claimed you'd stepped away from the keyboard and a friend had been playing a prank. The wonder of this was how reversible it was. It was like quantum physics. The words you'd typed were immediately deniable. If you didn't get the response you were hoping for, it had never happened.

---

54 *Silos*, as Michiko Kakutani calls them in her excellent *The Death of Truth*. Bubbles at least are transparent. Jia Tolentino is also excellent here in 'The I in Internet', published in her collection *Trick Mirror*.

If you'd told me back in 2001 that by 2020 the internet would have grown into an all-reaching, brain-changing superstructure, a human right that emboldens fascists, decides elections, enforces divisions and hosts a network of alternate realities, well, I wouldn't have heard you because I'd have been too busy trawling Nirvana lyrics for my new MSN screen name. But increasingly it's difficult to see the internet in its current form as a benevolent, even neutral, force. It's appropriate that the metaphor we arrived at so early on in the internet's development, the one that's outlasted all others,[55] is that of opening a window, since, like a window, the internet provides a narrow frame through which to see a world that must be walked through to be understood. At best it obfuscates as much as it elucidates – it tints our windows on the inside and out – and at its worst it's a hostile environment. Especially if you have the temerity (or misfortune) to stumble through it as a member of a minority.[56]

Back when Jews weren't allowed in tennis or golf clubs it was usually our names that gave us away, but with naturalisation and a trend towards acceptance there aren't many places left from which Jews are actively excluded. I said in the previous chapter that there are few spaces, physical and virtual, in which I feel unwelcome on account of my Jewishness but perhaps this was overstating the case.

You probably know this already but if you see a name encased in three sets of brackets on Twitter or somewhere else online it means the person the name belongs to is Jewish. Increasingly this is something a Jewish person might self-apply, usually in their screen name, and sometimes even non-Jews will use it to signal solidarity

---

55 When was the last time someone *surfed* the web or cruised down *the information superhighway*?

56 Or a woman.

with Jews, a sort of *I am Spartacus* for the digital age. The first time I saw a name encased in three brackets was in 2015. Back then it wasn't in someone's screen name but in a screen grab from a conversation on 4chan, one of the internet's most trafficked message boards, where the web still displays its lo-fi roots and Wild West spirit.

I don't remember what the conversation was about or why the screen grab caught my attention as I thumbed through my timeline in my usual morning fugue, but I suspect it had something to do with my first novel, *Ostrich*. The narrator of *Ostrich*, which had been published the year before, was a twelve-year-old boy with a tumour in his temporal lobe, and to capture his thoughts, which were non-chronological and full of digressions and sub-thoughts, a series of trapdoors for the reader to fall through, I'd taken to ordering them inside compound brackets, which often collapsed at the ends of sentences so that triple closing brackets were not uncommon. This technical innovation, I fondly imagined, was my small contribution to the Western canon, and such is the bottomlessness of my bottomless narcissism that when I first saw a name encased in three brackets, despite modest sales and mixed reviews, I thought my book had found its audience.

It was a double shock, then, to discover that the brackets had a different purpose altogether. They were the visual analogue for the echo sound effect that accompanied the pronouncement of Jewish names on the alt-right podcast *The Daily Shoah* (the Hebrew word for Holocaust). As its affiliate site *The Right Stuff* explains, 'All Jewish surnames echo throughout history. The echoes repeat the sad tale as they communicate the emotional lessons of our great white sins, imploring us to Never Forget the Six

Gorillion.'[57] But what had started as a cruel but not particularly notable joke among white supremacists soon took on a wider and more practical application. Unlike Google or most other search engines, Twitter allows non-numeric or non-alphabetic search terms. In other words, unlike Google, you can search its database for punctuation.

The triple brackets or 'echoes' as an anti-Semitic trope first breached mainstream consciousness in 2016 when Jonathan Weisman, the Washington editor for *The New York Times*, wrote a piece detailing his anti-Semitic trolling at the hands of Trump fans on Twitter. In the piece he recounts a bizarre exchange with the user @CyberTrump after Weisman had shared an essay by Robert Kagan on the emergence of fascism in America:

'The first tweet arrived as cryptic code, a signal to the army that I barely knew existed: "Hello (((Weisman)))."' Invited to explain – as Weisman writes, he'd intuited that the brackets around his surname referred to its Jewishness – his new friend was surprisingly forthcoming: 'It's a dog whistle, fool. Belling the cat for my fellow goyim.'

What followed will come as no surprise to anyone with even a cursory interest in the tropes and toolkits of online anti-Semites: pictures of hook-nosed Jews taken from Nazi propaganda posters, of gas ovens and the gates at Auschwitz (some with the legend *Arbeit Macht Frei* replaced with *Machen Amerika Great*); Holocaust revisionism; Holocaust denial; people lamenting that the Holocaust 'failed'. But what's notable isn't the specifics of the abuse (anti-Semites are about as original – and interchangeable – as a Fat Jewish Twitter caption) but the speed and number with which they arrived. As @CyberTrump, confused though he

---

57 A white supremacist/neo-Nazi term used to mock the number of Jews killed in the Holocaust.

was, had partially explained, this wasn't merely an old-fashioned dog whistle, the sort that gave cover to closet racists to privately stoke their backwards beliefs. It was a clarion call that circled them round a specific target. If Weisman was the cat and the racists the dogs, they were dogs being sicced on a particular vector. It wasn't a dog whistle in the traditional sense, in that it was designed only to be audible to fellow dogs,[58] it was a dog whistle in that it was meant to signal the start of an attack. It worked at once like a distinctive tag (say a yellow star) and a secret scent: one that at once identified the victim and stirred their attackers into a pheromonal frenzy.

Around the time of Jonathan Weisman's article in *The New York Times* a Google plug-in called Coincidence Detector was also coming to public awareness. Coincidence Detector was a growing database of Jewish people in public life and semi-public discourse as well as those with common Jewish names, which, once downloaded, would notify users when they were reading about Jews, or words written by Jews, or organisations deemed Jewish or sympathetic to Jews, by highlighting their names with the aforementioned echo. The purpose, according to the extension's description, was to help users 'detect total coincidences about who has been involved in certain political movements and media empires'.[59]

---

58 And deniable as racist to anyone calling it out.

59 In June 2016 it was widely reported that Google had removed the plug-in but a replica calling itself The Original (((Coincidence Detector))) remains downloadable for Chrome, Mozilla, Safari and Internet Explorer. Its copy encourages users to 'detect (((names))) for a reminder of what total coincidences have occurred in the past, and continue to occur today'. Alongside this is a *New York Times* piece on a legal case banning Confederate flags from car licence plates; a Forbes article about wealthy critics of Trump's rhetoric on immigration; and a Wikipedia entry for Neoconservatism.

What remains chilling about this, beyond the propagation of centuries-old racist tropes – the reason that when reading about it I felt like I'd been punched in the gut – was that its sole reason for existing was to directly reverse the choices made and actions taken by people like my grandfather when he'd changed his name from Greenbaum to Greene as a precaution against being singled out by those who wished him ill. If non-religious Jews could enjoy anonymity on the street and in the workplace, the equivalent was being revoked in the digital world, which increasingly played host to our personal and professional lives.

Before the publication of my first book, my publishers had given me a list of Twitter handles and told me to befriend as many as I could. I was given graphics that told me the best times to post and be online, and it was implied, quite strongly, that my professional success depended, in part, on maintaining an online presence. On being easy to find. I hadn't yet written about anti-Semitism or Jewish identity so I knew I had nothing personally to fear but any algorithm worth its salt could take one look at my syntax and how often I talked about *Seinfeld* or *Larry Sanders* and bolt me inside a triple-locked bracket. Also, gallingly, my anonymity was no longer implied by my identity but contingent on my relative lack of status and success. Say I reinvented myself as a vocal critic of Fred Perry polo shirts or sexism in videogames, would I be opening the floodgates to an ocean of racist abuse and harassment? Yes, I'm joking, but only in part. And because that's what Jews do.

And it was no longer true that the online world and the offline world were separate dimensions that impacted on each other only glancingly. Even in 2015 it had been a long time since anyone had used the initialism *IRL* to distinguish between life behind the keyboard and life away from it. The internet of 2015, unlike web 1.0, was not the rarefied realm of revocable confessions and non-canonical break-ups but a powerful superstructure that mapped on to the 'real' world, with the ability to spawn tangible consequences within it.

Another practice common among the alt-right was doxxing: the publishing of one's personal details, including phone numbers and addresses, and sometimes the addresses of the schools your kids were pupils at, on far-right and right-friendly message boards like Stormfront and 8chan. The result of having your name posted here was a lot more frightening than just online abuse. In 2017 a Jewish woman from Montana named Tanya Gersh made news worldwide when she sued the administrators of an online message board after she was subjected to months of threatening phone calls from white supremacists following publication of her personal details on a neo-Nazi website. Subscribers to the site promised to drive Gersh to suicide and threatened to organise an armed march through her town. 'I once answered the phone and all I heard were gunshots,' Gersh told reporters.[60] 'There were endless references to being thrown in the oven, being gassed.' As part of the coordinated campaign of harassment, neo-Nazis also contacted her employers alleging illegal conduct, and posted pictures online of her twelve-year-old son, photoshopped over images from concentration camps, alongside the address of his school.[61]

In one chilling historical parallel, Gersh returned home one day to find her husband sitting in a dark house with suitcases packed. As Gersh explains: 'This was so far beyond harassment. This was really terrorism.' Indeed, the site responsible, *The Daily*

---

60 As reported in the *Guardian* ('Jewish woman in Montana sues over "troll-storm" of neo-Nazi harassment').

61 Gersh's son too was targeted by online abusers. A sample message: 'Psst kid, there's a free Xbox One inside this oven.'

Stormer, had been read by at least three confirmed far-right terrorists: Dylann Roof, who murdered nine black congregants of a historic African American church in Charleston; Thomas Mair, who murdered the MP Jo Cox; and James Jackson, who stabbed to death a randomly selected black man on a New York street the month before Gersh's troll-storm made landfall. Gersh had legitimate cause to fear for her life and the lives of her family. And the attack has had lasting effects: she was forced to quit her job as an estate agent for fear of subjecting her clients to harassment, she sees a trauma therapist twice a week, suffers from crippling anxiety and 'often falls asleep and wakes up weeping'. Gersh's case is remarkable only because she pursued her abusers through the courts. There are many other victims whose names we don't know and *The Daily Stormer*, who were eventually ordered to pay a large amount in damages, is just the tip of a very white iceberg.

But something needn't threaten your life or even your physical safety to have a significant and adverse effect on your mental health and online experience, and chiefly this is not an essay about how Jews are put in fear for their lives by far-right racists online. Rather, it's about a particular characteristic of the internet and how this intersects with the particular character of anti-Semitism, and why, after thousands of years as an itinerant, free-floating political philosophy, in the quantum, infinitely mirrored hallway of the internet anti-Semitism (that most quantum of hatreds) may finally have found its natural home. It's about the importance of safe spaces not just on college campuses but in intellectual domains and within cultural movements, and how hard they are for Jews to find.

As Kakutani writes in *The Death of Truth*, her treatise on how the internet, the news cycle and the bad-faith co-opting of postmodernist theory about the instability of language have led us to the anteroom of a new kind of totalitarianism, the internet is decreasingly a window and increasingly a mirror. It's no longer the case, as at its inception, that the World Wide Web is a searchable database of human knowledge. Instead it's a portal into our own subconscious. The internet is hungry for data and, as capitalism conquers the final frontier of the self, we've provided it in spades and (mostly) without coercion: through our search histories, our Facebook likes, the amount of time we spend on certain websites, and the items forgotten at the bottom of our shopping carts.

With this data the internet has built a picture of who it believes us to be – crucially, of who we believe *ourselves* to be. When we search Google, then, we get a personalised experience. The ordering of results – or the results we're shown – depends not just (not even primarily) on their relevance to the search terms we've typed but on the pointillist portrait we've already provided through our previous searches and historic behaviour. The results are likely to be pleasing to this self-image – that is to say agreeable with it – since the longer we spend on a site and the more content we share, the more valuable we are to advertisers who still make up the bulk of the internet's cash flow.

This is the attention economy and it has had several key consequences. Chief among them, though, is the erosion of objective truth. As news becomes entertainment, and algorithms become increasingly adept at delivering us the content we find most entertaining, the walls around each of us have grown taller. Through the promise of connecting us with like-minded people, the internet has filtered out interactions with those we disagree with (or limited it to the level of trolling). Not only this, it's insulated us from information that might challenge our pre-held notions and made it impossible to know what facts we share with our political opponents and which are exclusive to our own small communities.

What I've just described is a perfect incubator for conspiratorial thinking. Often the conspiracies the internet produces are benign, even amusing. A subset of One Direction fans, for example, are committed to the appealing theory that Harry and Louis are a romantic couple, a fact suppressed by their management to protect their appeal to their largely straight female audience.[62] But just as often they're not. When Edgar Maddison Welch walked into a Washington pizza parlour on 4 December 2016 and fired three shots with an assault rifle, it was the result of months of Twitter posts and message board threads about a secret child sex ring theorists had 'uncovered' by decoding food-related code words in the hacked emails of Hillary Clinton's campaign manager, John Podesta.[63]

But benign or otherwise, all conspiracy theories have something significant in common: they are all inherently undisprovable. To those distrustful of deep states and professional journalists, any refutation can be dismissed as a diversion or as part of a cover-up. The refutation becomes proof itself: of how close the theorist has come to uncovering the truth, of just how deep this thing goes. This is beyond confirmation bias into something more extreme. No matter the evidence presented, proponents can't be dissuaded and proof to the contrary only strengthens belief.

---

62 The theory even has a name: 'Larry Stylinson'.
63 The fictitious ring, which was said to involve Hillary Clinton and the Obamas, had been popularised by alt-right 4chan users and later reported on in several Turkish daily papers.

In January 2016 when Louis Tomlinson's partner gave birth to his first child, fans theorised that the baby was a robot since the existence of a baby born from Louis's heterosexual relationship was incompatible with his commitment to Harry. In this way the baby became confirmatory of the pre-existing conspiracy and was incorporated into it. Speaking after his arrest, Edgar Welch regretted his handling of his 'investigation' but declined to dismiss the theory it was born from, rejecting its description as 'fake news'.[64] Challenging a conspiracy theorist, even with evidence that appears empirical, will only embolden them. A conspiracy theory is a one-man human centipede: endlessly feeding on its own cycle of infinitely reconstituted shit. Conspiracy is self-sustaining. It's self-generative.

All of which brings us back round to the Jews. As discussed previously, our history of persecution, our statelessness, quantum strength–weakness, our privilege and our perceived success, have long made Jews perfect fodder for conspiracy. Jews have been blamed for everything from 9/11 to modern art (which Hitler felt was a Jewish plot to undermine the German spirit). There's an argument to be made that the first-ever conspiracy theory was anti-Semitic: a literary forgery from Tsarist Russia called *The Protocols of the Elders of Zion* that claimed to expose the Jewish plot for world domination, and is still cited today. Jews are so slippery, so notoriously hard to pin down in our nature, that we're blamed simultaneously for the creations of both communism and capitalism – which goes some way to explaining why certain anti-Jewish tropes are met so uncritically on the left. In recent years, though, facilitated by this growing conspiratorial bent, certain anti-Jewish conspiracies have

---

64 Some theorists speculated that the shooting was staged, a false-flag operation intended to discredit the investigation.

been repopularised, reaching new audiences, and in many cases turbocharged.

One of the more extreme recent examples of anti-Jewish conspiracy can be found in the work of the conspiracy theorist David Icke. A professional lunatic and former sports reporter who in 1991 went on *Wogan*, dressed in a pink-and-green shell suit, to discuss claims (his) that he was the son of God. A man who believes the Queen Mother belonged to a race of interdimensional shape-shifting reptiles,[65] Icke has seen something of a resurgence in respectability in recent years. No longer the punchline he was for most of the nineties, Icke has spent much of the past two decades selling out venues around the world, talking, sometimes for up to ten hours, to audiences eager to hear about how their lives are governed by a shadowy global elite intent on maintaining their subservience.

In a transnational age in which democracy is threatened by encroaching fascism and the shrinking relevance of the nation state, and pan-national corporations mine the Arctic and colonise rainfall, it's not hard to understand the appeal,[66] but Icke's conclusions are straight out of the fantasist's playbook. Not only are there the interdimensional lizards, now human–lizard hybrids, who shape world events to keep humans in a state of perpetual fear so they might feed off the 'negative energy' this produces, there's their template for world domination, which is set out in *The Protocols of the Elders of Zion*. It's worth stating that Icke maintains he's not anti-Semitic and that similarities between his interdimensional lizard people, who first appeared in the Middle East around six thousand years ago, and any ancient tribes that come to mind are just

---

65 Really. His Wikipedia entry is a fucking ride.

66 Indeed, there's an argument that conspiracy theories are our age's folklore, articulating the fears we feel but are unable to accurately diagnose.

coincidence, but Jews have long been depicted as half-human, often part-lizard, and the lizard people he's exposed have been disproportionately Jewish. Plus there's the weird tell of hiding Stars of David in his PowerPoint presentations explaining the interconnectedness of the superpowers that rule over us.

In recent years, though, Icke has shifted his interest away from interdimensional reptiles to what he calls Rothschild Zionists. In his own words, speaking in 2014, Rothschild Zionism 'was created as a secret society within the web to massively contribute to the manipulation and control of our global society and individual countries et cetera et cetera'. So another conspiracy, amusingly vague and structurally similar to the first, but this time the baddies aren't prominent Jewish amphibians but prominent Zionists, Jewish and otherwise. Icke has repeatedly been accused of anti-Semitism and Holocaust denial,[67] and while it's possible he really does believe that actual blood-drinking lizards run the world, the anti-Semites certainly believe he's an anti-Semite: he's held in high esteem by both the far and alt-right and counts among his audience neo-Nazi militias like the terrorist group Combat 18.

It's telling that Icke can fill out theatres the world over with his Partridge-brand fever dreams, but what's more illuminating – more frightening and infuriating – is what happened in November 2018 when a video detailing and condemning his questionable rhetoric was released on Twitter by Momentum, the left-wing grassroots political organisation credited with lifting Jeremy Corbyn to leadership of the Labour party. Within seconds the responses came.

---

67   In his 1995 book *And the Truth Shall Set You Free*, Icke alleges that a 'small Jewish clique' financed Hitler's rise to power in 1933. This same clique, he alleges, is responsible for the First World War, the Second World War and the Russian Revolution. In the same book he rails against the suppression of 'alternative information' to the 'official line' on the Second World War and the Holocaust.

Some of them were supportive, but most were critical, furious, as followers rushed to Icke's defence. As one supporter who now threatened to cancel their Momentum membership put it, it was clear the group had been infiltrated by Zionists. How else to explain their disapproval of Icke? In the words of another, Momentum were attempting to commit political suicide 'as far as being a socialist organisation is concerned'.

You might think it strange that members of a left-wing, anti-racist activist group would rush to the defence of a speaker whose talks are attended by neo-Nazis and who propagates theories that would have sat quite comfortably in *Mein Kampf*, but if you do you probably haven't been following British politics for the last few years (how jealous I am). To many it can seem odd, even suspiciously so, that the avowedly anti-racist left should be the subject of an ever-rolling scandal about the unequal treatment of Jews two decades into the twenty-first century, especially in the run-up to an election. To others, though, this is proof of the biggest conspiracy of all. As Icke himself puts it, those who get closest to the truth face assassination, either of themselves or their character, and to many on the left the constant reports of anti-Semitic posts and outbursts by members of their community isn't emblematic of a deep cultural problem that needs urgently to be understood and addressed, but proof that Jews (and a powerful Jewish lobby) assert disproportionate control over the news agenda.

So far in this book I've tried to avoid talking about specific political parties because anti-Semitism is not confined to any one point on the political spectrum and because Jewish experience is not (or not entirely) defined by anti-Semitism, but it's impossible to go further without addressing the scandal that has embroiled the British Labour party since 2015. The question that dominated the British print and broadcast media for much of 2016–19, of whether or not Jeremy Corbyn, leader of the Labour party from 2015, was an anti-Semite, is not one I'm particularly interested in answering since a) I'll convince no one, and b) it's not the right one to be asking (although you can find my thoughts at the end of this book[i]), but it's certainly true that there is a deep problem in the culture of the Labour party – and the left at large – that allows such hatred to flourish and take root, a problem that mirrors and is exacerbated by the vectors information travels in online and relies on conspiratorial ideas about Jewish identity that were old when God was young. This is best demonstrated when – as we increasingly find ourselves doing – Jews on the left raise concerns about anti-Semitism. Generally, one or more of three things happen:

1. Our loyalty is questioned and an agenda assumed. We're secret Tories or secret centralists, looking to subvert a progressive socialist movement that threatens our status. This is anti-Semitic for two reasons, firstly because it assumes Jews have split loyalties and can't be taken at our word (we're sometimes also assumed to be secret Zionists), and because it posits a view of Jewishness that is somehow incompatible with socialist values.

2. We're assured that whatever we've complained about is not anti-Semitic. The suggestion here being that our experience as Jews disqualifies us from thinking rationally and objectively on the subject. The culprit's intent (or anti-racist credentials) is privileged over the effect on the victim, the implication being that we're oversensitive and primed to be offended. The term here would be gaslighting.

3. We're asked to provide evidence.

Of these three the third would appear the most reasonable and it's what happened to me in 2018 when a friend of a friend, on discovering I was Jewish, asked me, well-meaningly, what I thought about an anti-Semitic mural that Jeremy Corbyn had defended on Facebook. The mural depicted a group of six white bankers playing a Monopoly-like board game on the bowed backs of naked black workers under an all-seeing Masonic eye, and had made news after comments had emerged from 2012 in which Corbyn had defended the artist and argued against its removal. How could this mural be anti-Semitic, my acquaintance wanted to know, when only two of the bankers depicted were Jewish?

Looking back, I should've asked my acquaintance how he knew which two bankers were Jewish (might it have something to do with the hook noses, the narrow-set eyes, and the way one was sweatily clutching a wad of cash – all right-wing racist tropes) but instead I floundered. I tried to explain that anti-Semitism was something that sometimes requires knowledge of certain tropes to spot, that people need education, that sometimes it's easier to sense than describe, but I could tell as I was saying it that I was losing him. From my current vantage I'm angry with myself for not arguing harder, explaining better, but I'm only angry because I've since had so much practice. It's a pattern that repeats itself endlessly, both online and off: people who'd never dream of asking a trans person why something was transphobic or an Asian woman why something was racist constantly ask Jews to explain anti-Semitism, with the implication that it's down to us to convince them it's real.

But herein lies the problem: if you don't accept the premise that anti-Semitism exists as a problem that needs to be addressed – and not solely a rhetorical weapon wielded by the media and your political opponents – then no amount of evidence is permissible, since it's written in a language you refuse to learn. Here, then, is another solo human centipede: accusations of anti-Semitism are a manifestation of Jewish mendacity or of Jewish paranoia.

But, as my MSN screen name surely once read, just because you're paranoid, don't mean they're not out to get you. Witness, for example, what happens when Jews do provide evidence. After the Jewish and former Labour MP Luciana Berger spoke at length in Parliament detailing the anti-Semitic abuse she'd received in her eighteen-year career as a politician, with a particular uptick after Corbyn's election to leader, she was accused of lying about needing police protection during the 2018 Labour party conference. In the run-up to the conference Berger had received several death threats and a barrage of online abuse, most of it anti-Semitic in nature, some of it so extreme that the posters were prosecuted for hate crimes, but when commenters online decided that pictures from the event, which clearly showed her flanked by members of the Merseyside constabulary, had been doctored, another conspiracy was born. Berger had revealed her true agenda: in speaking out on her experiences of anti-Semitism she was attempting to deflect from legitimate criticism of Israel. Like Louis Tomlinson's robot baby the pictures proved precisely what they aimed to suppress.

Similarly, in 2016, at the launch of Lady Chakrabarti's report on anti-Semitism, Ruth Smeeth, another Jewish Labour MP who'd spoken extensively on the issue, was accused by an activist of working 'hand in hand' with the right-wing press in a plot to oust Corbyn from his post. The activist, Marc Wadsworth, was later expelled by the party's National Constitution Committee but he maintained at his hearing that he was 'totally and utterly opposed to anti-Semitism'. Meanwhile, after leaving the launch in the wake of Wadsworth's abuse, Ruth Smeeth was the subject of over 25,000 abusive messages and posts on social media, including several calling her a 'Mossad informant', a 'fucking traitor', and a 'yid cunt'.[68]

What this amounts to, of course, is a secondary wave of emotional abuse. It's a form of gaslighting that extracts a further psychological toll and makes Jews uncertain about coming forward. In intent it may not always be malicious but this hardly matters. And like much contemporary left-wing anti-Semitism, in its reliance on the presumption of Jewish paranoia it recalls tactics employed on the far and alt-right to undermine the legitimacy of Jewish concerns.

In November 2018, with the echo tag having seeped into the mainstream,[69] alt-right 8chan users suggested wishing Jews a 'Happy Hanukkah' as a way of tagging them online. This came with the same deniability that had initially recommended the triple brackets but also the added bonus that it appeared friendly, so that Jews reporting the tags would be made to look unreasonable and ridiculous. Here, then, was a suggestion designed to delegitimise concerns about anti-Semitism and discredit those making them while simultaneously furthering a campaign of intimidation against Jews. That this could equally describe the treatment of Smeeth and Berger by some in their party should appal everyone and surprise no one. After all, this is the Jews, who are not afforded the same protections on the left as other minorities deemed more archetypal.

Still, though, there will be those who require more evidence before they're convinced. While writing a first draft of this essay in December 2018, I logged on to Twitter to find that the then Labour MP Chris Williamson had shared a petition in support of a jazz musician called Gilad Atzmon, who had been banned

---

68 As reported by the Jewish Labour Movement in their 2019 submission to the Equality and Human Rights Commission.

69 Even Nazi culture gets appropriated.

from a venue by Islington Council. Gilad Atzmon is an ex-Jewish anti-Semite who in 2008 was disavowed by the activist group Jews Against Zionism for 'crossing the red line from antisemitism to Holocaust denial'.

A selection of his choicest quotes: 'I'm not going to say if it's right to burn down a synagogue, I can see it's a rational act'; 'We must begin to take the accusation that Jewish people are trying to control the world very seriously'; 'The Jewish tribal mindset – left, right, centre – sets Jews apart from humanity'; 'Jewish ideology is driving our planet into a catastrophe'; 'American Jewry makes any debate on whether *The Protocols of the Elders of Zion* is an authentic document or rather a forgery irrelevant. American Jews do control the world.' (From a cursory search of his Twitter: 'I despise the Jew in me and I detest the Jew in you' . . .)

Taken in isolation it's conceivable Williamson was unaware of Atzmon's political leanings when he signed and shared the petition in his defence but Williamson has form here that makes this explanation difficult and deserves examining. In February 2019 Williamson was suspended from the Labour party for telling attendees of a Momentum meeting that the party had been 'too apologetic' over accusations of anti-Semitism (which in 2017 he called 'sinister', a 'proxy war' and a 'dirty, low-down trick') and eventually encouraged to resign, but not before he'd been praised by the Leader's Office as a model MP and devoted anti-racist. Here, then, are a few of his greatest hits.

In June 2018 Williamson defended Peter Willsman, a member of Labour's National Executive, over claims Willsman had made that British Jews were 'Trump fanatics'. In August of the same year he defended Cyril Chilson, expelled from Labour for tweeting about 'Jew funding' of the Tories. In April 2018 he defended an expelled Labour member who'd tweeted about

'Jewish companies' with 'Jewish blood' that 'oppress global workers'. In October 2018, hours after the Pittsburgh synagogue shooting, he trolled the Board of Deputies of British Jews by accusing them of using anti-Semitic tropes. In June 2019 he promoted the work of Pedro Baños, an anti-Semitic conspiracy theorist (published by Penguin), and propagated a conspiracy theory that an organisation called the Integrity Initiative was undermining Spanish democracy by preventing Baños's appointment as national security advisor. Since 2016 he has repeatedly cited the work of Alfred-Maurice de Zayas, a hero to Holocaust deniers for his accounts of Nazi Germany which have frequently been described as revisionist, and board member of the Desiderius-Erasmus-Stiftung, a foundation established by Germany's far-right AfD (who we'll return to shortly). In June 2018 Williamson responded to reports of anti-Semitism in the Oxford University Labour Club, which included claims made in front of Jewish students that Auschwitz was a 'cash cow', by dismissing them out of hand and changing the topic to Israel.

In his resignation letter Williamson attempted to settle the debate over whether or not he's anti-Semitic, referring to the calls for him to resign as a 'witch hunt' brought by 'apartheid apologists' who 'shroud themselves under the banner of socialism' and 'influenc[e] Labour's foreign and domestic policy' while 'serv[ing] the objectives of far-right activists'. He also repeats claims that all accusations of anti-Semitism against him and Labour in general are 'smears' and 'unfounded'. He goes on to refer to the Jewish Labour Movement as '*Po'ale Zion*' and describes Labour's partial acknowledgement of its issues with anti-Semitism as a 'capitulation'.

Again, to Jews on the left who've had the misfortune to follow this in real time, none of this is particularly surprising, but what is alarming in this letter is Williamson's claim that its addressee,

Jennie Formby, shares his beliefs that accusations against him are 'smears' and 'unfounded'. Jennie Formby was appointed Labour's General Secretary in 2018, with the party under investigation from the Equality and Human Rights Commission over allegations of institutional racism (that charge coined in the Macpherson Report to label police conduct in the wake of the Stephen Lawrence investigation).[70] In her role as General Secretary, as alleged in the BBC's 2019 *Panorama* investigation into Labour anti-Semitism, Formby, along with the Leader's Office, assumed oversight of the disciplinary process charged with investigating accusations of anti-Semitism and enforcing the party's 'zero tolerance' stance on the issue. Party whistle-blowers – who after the programme aired were, of course, systematically discredited – allege that on several occasions she overruled decisions and downgraded punishments: expulsions to suspensions; suspensions to 'slaps on the wrist'. She is also accused of deleting emails relating to cases.

But hasn't all this become horribly politicised and am I not in danger of simply parroting Conservative and *Daily Mail* talking points? Well, yes. Perhaps the most nauseating quirk of our current political crisis is the Tories' selective outrage on anti-Jewish racism, a phenomenon that further alienates Jews even while claiming to amplify our voices. This selective outrage is particularly hard to take, seriously or otherwise, when their own frontbenchers, like Leader of the House and anthropomorphised hatstand Jacob Rees-Mogg, are happy to associate with far-right anti-Semites like

---

70 Labour is only the second political party ever to be investigated for institutional racism by the EHRC. The other is the British National Party.

Germany's Alternative für Deutschland, whose anti-Jewish rhetoric[71] has coincided with a sharp rise in hate crimes against German Jews and is believed by many to have inspired a terror attack in Halle in October 2019 in which a neo-Nazi gunman killed two passers-by after attempting to storm a synagogue in which congregants were gathered to observe Yom Kippur.

In September 2019, in his first Prime Minister's Questions session, Boris Johnson, who has his own charge sheet on anti-Semitism, was handed the chance to apologise for his own appalling record of racist rhetoric, which includes calling Africans 'piccaninnies with watermelon smiles' and comparing Muslim women to 'letterboxes' (supposedly in service of defending liberal values). Rather than apologise for his words, the effect they've had,[72] or at the bare minimum the offence caused, Johnson chose to attack the opposition for its failure to offer Jewish voters adequate assurances that its own problems were in hand. This kind of sophistry, which may be Johnson's one political skill, is worse than disingenuous since it converts Jewish hurt and legitimate concern to political backspin, a defensive measure employed by a government who have nothing positive to offer. Furthermore, it drives a wedge between Jews and other minorities or victims of abuse, and invites them (and others) to associate Jews with the party of Windrush, of Grenfell, of Enoch Powell, of Brexit, of the Hostile Environment. This is sickening on its own terms but harder to take still when you consider the Tory party's own record on anti-Jewish hatred.

---

71 For example, a call to ban the kosher preparation of meat and the description of German Nazism as 'a speck of bird poop' in the nation's history.

72 Like the AfD's, Johnson's rhetoric has been widely cited as a factor in rising hate crimes.

In the run-up to the December 2019 General Election, two Tory candidates were suspended from the party for making anti-Semitic comments: one for calling British Jews 'brainwashed' by Israel, the other for claiming that 'some of the events [of the Holocaust are] fabricated'. A further three candidates were investigated but not suspended: Sally-Ann Hart, now Member of Parliament for Hastings and Rye, for sharing a video suggesting George Soros controlled the EU and liking a Nazi slogan on Facebook; Lee Anderson, now MP for Ashford, for being an active member of a Facebook group that promotes anti-Soros conspiracy theories; and Richard Short, who lost in St Helens South and Whiston, for asking a Jewish journalist if she was more loyal to the UK or to Israel.

And let's return for a moment to the prime minister himself. While editor of the *Spectator* from 1999 to 2005, Johnson was comfortable enough with anti-Semitism to employ the right-wing commentator Taki Theodoracopulos, who could recently be found writing paeans to the 'heroism' of German soldiers fighting in the Second World War and defences of Greece's neo-Nazi Golden Dawn, and who in 2001 (the middle of Johnson's tenure) wrote a piece so extreme in its anti-Jewish rhetoric that it prompted the magazine's owner, Conrad Black, to compare him to Goebbels.

Meanwhile, across the Atlantic, Donald Trump favours the same playbook, using his support of Israel and often his daughter Ivanka and son-in-law Jared Kushner as a shrivelled fig leaf of deniability in the face of mounting evidence of his own rampant and blatant racism. In July 2019, after Trump had tweeted that four Democratic congresswomen of colour should 'go back' to the 'countries they came from' (not exactly subtle stuff; more the kind of racism that gets drunken uncles uninvited from family weddings), the leader of the free world hid behind his most loyal and media-savvy attack dog Kellyanne Conway, who answered a Jewish reporter's question by demanding his ethnicity. It shouldn't need stating how dangerous and irrelevant such a question was but that the reporter turned out to be Jewish played, infuriatingly, into the White House's hands. Conway later tweeted a further defence against charges of her own racist rhetoric by attacking Ilhan Omar, one of the congresswomen Trump had tweeted at. In February 2019 Omar had apologised unreservedly for a tweet that employed an anti-Semitic trope in reference to a pro-Israeli lobby group, and in labelling her a racist Conway was able to sidestep endlessly provable allegations into her own conduct. Again, then, Jewish hurt was mobilised to defend racists and, bizarrely, signal their anti-racist credentials. It reminds me of Chris Finch's claim in the UK version of *The Office* that he can't be a misogynist since his mum's a woman. *How can I hate minorities? My favourite shield's one.*

This is what people on the left mean when they say anti-Semitism has been *weaponised*, and this is both obviously true and dangerously adjacent to claims that it's a smear or has all been invented. In an age of increasing partisanship (which again is attributable to the internet and its economy of attention) most things are decided along party lines. My enemy's enemy might not be my friend but my enemy's friend is most certainly my enemy, and it can be difficult to think beyond this into more nuanced terms. In this way, the right's faux-concern about anti-Semitism others Jews within the category of 'other', further removing the protections of the anti-racist left. This is not a deliberate ploy on behalf of the right but acceptable collateral since Jewish feelings of security, like those of all minorities, are readily expendable.

Just because the right champion our hurt when it's politically expedient for them to do so does not mean that they offer Jews a home. It should hardly need saying, and in saner times it wouldn't, but Jews and racists do not make good friends. Trump's and Johnson's willingness to cheapen our anguish to avoid account-ability ironically proves this beyond doubt. And anti-racism is only as strong as its weakest link. You can't oppose anti-Semitism and call Mexicans rapists, deport citizens because they're West Indian or separate children from their parents and put them in cages. All of those things devalue non-white lives and, by extension, the lives of Jews.

◆　◆　◆

Yes, all of this is infuriating, frightening, triggering, depressing, circular, never-ending . . .

But more than this, it's exhausting. It's not just the constant calls to provide evidence of discrimination, or the second-guessing of yourself that comes from so rarely being taken at your word, it's the fact that the conversation never seems to evolve. If there's one thing you take away from this book about what it's like to be Jewish in 2020, it's that mostly we're tired. We're tired of conversations that start out about anti-Semitism and end up about Israel, we're tired of having to prove we're under threat to people who don't want to see proof, we're tired of accusations our concerns are coordinated for political gain and that we're in cahoots with those who are only too happy to profit from our pain. We're tired of having to assure you we're the right kind of Jew before our thoughts can be aired; of needing to justify why something's caused us offence and not being considered authorities on racism against us; of being accused of being insular – as Churchill put it, of 'refusing to absorb' – by the same people who seem unwilling or unable to understand or appre-ciate the particularities of our experience. We're tired of people who only have the bandwidth to care about anti-Semitism or 'real racism', as if the two were somehow exclusive and in acknowledging the latter you draw funds from the former. We're tired of people who only care about anti-Semitism when it's in their opponent's party and is politically useful. We're tired of being disappointed by people we once liked or respected (Ken Loach,[73] Billy Bragg,[74] Alice Walker,[75] Gary Oldman[76]). We're tired of having to forgive or disqualify our childhood idols.[77] We're tired of constantly being left wanting and always teetering on the brink of thinking it would be better if we just shut up and put up since there are bigger fish to fry. We're tired of waiting for solidarity like the kid who played Reese

---

73 On whether Holocaust denial is acceptable: 'History is for all of us to discuss. All history is our common heritage to discuss and analyse. The founding of the State of Israel, for example, based on ethnic cleansing, is there for us to discuss.' When given the chance to clarify: 'Exaggerated or false charges of anti-Semitism have coincided with the election of Jeremy Corbyn as leader . . . Discredit his supporters and you weaken his leadership . . . We will not be intimidated.'

74 Asked to clarify comments that British Jews had 'work to do' to repair relations with the Labour party: 'If they want to build trust, I do [think they have work to do] . . . It takes two to tango.'

75 On David Icke: 'I believe he is brave enough to ask the questions others fear to ask.' Plus her poem 'It Is Our (Frightful) Duty to Study the Talmud', in which she attributes Palestinian oppression, conditions in American prisons, and war in general to Jewish scripture, all while defending her right to criticise Israel without accusations of anti-Semitism.

76 In 2014, on Mel Gibson's drunken 2006 anti-Jewish tirade in which he claimed Jews were responsible for all the wars in the world: 'Take a fucking joke . . . We've all said those things . . . Mel is in a town that's run by Jews and he said the wrong thing, he's bitten the hand that I guess has fed him.'

77 Roald Dahl: 'There is a trait in the Jewish character that does provoke animosity . . . I mean there is always a reason why anti-anything crops up; even a stinker like Hitler didn't pick on them for no reason.' (That word *stinker*, like something Wodehouse would use to describe a meddling aunt.)

waiting for a reboot of *Malcolm in the Middle* – and, personally, of having to make this funny so you'll listen.

Believe us – *believe us* – however tired you are of hearing about anti-Semitism, we're more tired of talking about it. Most of all, we're tired of trying to convince people that all of this is happening. Only that's not quite it, or that's only part of it. We're tired of trying to convince them that it's happening and it matters.

At the conception of this book, I wondered if my son would choose to identify as Jewish but the truth is that increasingly I'm far more worried that the choice of his Jewishness will be imposed on him. That this is a concern a parent should have in 2020 is, of course, absurd, but acknowledging its absurdity doesn't automatically make a situation improve. For things to get better, for anti-Semitism to decline, or at least to shrink back into the shadows as the shameful, senseless hatred it is, we need education. But we need education that doesn't rely on Jews to convince us of its necessity. It's too much to ask that Jews endure anti-Semitism and are left with the burden of proving it exists, especially when so many requests to do this are made in bad faith. Maybe it's true that understanding anti-Semitism requires a little more nuance or historical knowledge than understanding other forms of racism, but unless the patience to acquire this can be found, Jews will continue to feel unsupported and disenfranchised – and, at the extreme end, their lives will be endangered.

I told you earlier in this book that to understand Judaism you had to look to the pronouns and the same is true, I think, of Jewishness itself. That even now I can't decide between *us* and *them* should illustrate a little about the complexities and contradictions of British Jewish (*anything* Jewish) identity. On a good week I can go days at a time without thinking about how I'm Jewish, but the good weeks are getting shorter and further apart. It shouldn't matter which you put first – Jewish Brits or British Jews – Jews should feel comfortable expressing their Jewishness online and off, in our lives, our work, our homes, our communities and our places of worship. That increasingly we're not is a stain on us all, one that, infuriatingly, should shine some light on why a vast majority of British Jews, while rejecting the definition imposed by popular discourse, would identify as some shade of Zionist.[78]

But this hasn't been an essay about Jewish statehood and I won't end with an allusion to something I consider, at most, peripheral to my Jewish identity. Instead, here's a story my dad told me once. My parents are divorced and my dad is non-practising – sometimes it seems that Jewishness is one of the things he lost in the settlement – but from the age of eleven to fifteen, when he was asked to leave, he attended a Jewish secondary school in North London. One of its rules was that pupils wear skullcaps not just on school grounds but whenever they were in uniform. This meant that every morning my dad and his younger brother had to run a gauntlet. They'd be picked on at the bus stop or the walk to and from it, on a good day insulted, on a bad day spat at. One day someone threw a bottle at my dad and struck him above the eye. Although this in itself wasn't unusual, this time my dad retaliated by picking up a stone and throwing it back. I can imagine my grandma's response when my dad and his brother got home, the fuss she would have made – ammonia and butterfly stitches, one-handed with the other fluttering permanently in front of her chest. When my grandpa Cyril, who'd changed his name from Greenbaum to Greene but sent both his sons to a Jewish school, came home, sympathy was in short supply. What happened? he demanded to know, and proudly my dad told him: *I got one of*

---

78   90% of those consulted in a 2015 survey by Yachad, a Jewish advocacy group working for a political solution to the conflict, support the right of Israel to exist as a Jewish state.

them back. My grandpa wasn't a violent man, though he'd played rugby for the navy and had the build of someone you wouldn't want to upset, so he didn't hit my dad, but by the time he was done my dad wished that he had. 'Never,' he told him. 'Never give them an excuse.'

Which reminds me now of another memory, this one my own (and yes, I realise we're no longer talking about the internet). Before I graduated to playing in the Jewish-only London Maccabi football league, I played on Sunday lunchtimes, after cheder, for a non-Jewish side in the disproportionately Jewish suburb I grew up in. The squad, which was twenty or so strong, had five Jewish players, which was enough to make us known as the league's Jewish team. There were often comments – sometimes friendly, sometimes not, rarely memorable – and one Sunday in late summer we played an away game at a pitch that backed on to a pub garden. I was eight or nine years old, too young to know that pubs served alcohol and alcohol made people say what they thought, and I had no reason to suspect this game would be different from any other. The only difference was that for once my dad, our literal twelfth man, wasn't the only dad on the touchline.

Parents of the opposition lined up at the border of the pitch and the pub's picket fence. Among them – possibly parents, possibly onlookers – were several pub-goers who'd started early. They were the sort of men impossible not to reduce to their most elemental features: their multiple necks, too-tight polos and suntans that confused small animals into thinking it was nightfall – the sort of men that would be made of straw if they weren't so instantly recognisable to anyone who's ever played Sunday league football on a pitch that backs on to a pub. I was playing in central midfield, as far from the touchline as it was possible to be, so at first I was only vaguely aware of the laughter and chanting wafting into play from not long after the game began. But midway through the first half I went over to take a throw-in and was met by a gesture that even I knew. One of the pinkest men in the pinkest shirt raised his right arm and, laughing, stamped his feet. A few minutes later our right-back stopped to pick up something that had been thrown at his feet.

A shiny 10p piece.

The game continued and I remained absorbed in it but I was aware in my periphery of my father, all five foot eight of him, striding over to confront the men in their pink polos. I can see him now as I write this, removing his glasses as if he expected to be punched. And I can still remember, like a cold metal flower, the feeling of shame that opened up inside of me. How? How could he be so embarrassingly literal? Couldn't he tell when something was meant as a joke?

It's taken twenty-five years and becoming a parent for me to understand these stories and to begin to comprehend my father's anger and my grandfather's fear. In a sense I'm grateful to the men on the touchline, just as I'm grateful to the racists on 4chan and Twitter who post their bile on public forums, for opening my eyes to what was there all along. For whatever reason, for any reason, for no reason at all, to be Jewish is to live with the knowledge that no matter who you are or what you do there are people who will hate you. For Jews like me who were born at the end of history on to a tiny island of temporal privilege in which there were no ghettos to house us, no prohibitions on our movements, religious expressions or entry into professions, no pogroms to drive us from our homes and no camps to mechanise our mass murder, this can be a hard fact to grasp and an even harder one to accept.

Personally, it's taken me thirty-four years. I still don't fear for my safety or sleep with a packed suitcase under my bed, and I do still feel that Jews have less to navigate than some other minorities who don't get the choice of when and how to disclose their minority status (although if I were visibly Jewish I might feel differently, and this would be a different book), but I no longer think that my parents were ridiculous to prepare me for a world that might not fully accept me for who I am. For many Jews of my generation, it can still feel like we're living outside of history, and while I don't believe that history's repeating, that we're in credible danger of internment or expulsion in anything other than virtual terms, it does feel a lot like that island of privilege is eroding and history is starting to crank back up again.

Chapter Eight:
Poland

Among the atrocities, inhumanities and crimes against nature perpetrated by the Nazis, ruining my birthday ranks, I realise, fairly low. Nevertheless, as my alarm sounds at quarter to six, I can't help but summon a fresh wave of resentment. Two nights ago I kissed goodbye to my family – I told Arthur, whom I'd never spent a night away from, that I was off on a chocolate run – and boarded a train from my home in Crystal Palace to North London, land of my forefathers, to sleep on a friend's sofa for onward transit to Heathrow and then Warsaw. The hour of the flight was, appropriately enough, ungodly. There's a great joke about a Holocaust survivor who gets to heaven and tells God a Holocaust joke. 'That's not funny,' God chastises him, to which the survivor shrugs. 'Yeah, I guess you had to be there.' The implication being, He wasn't.

After breakfast (a hard-boiled egg, foamy apple and lukewarm tea in a polystyrene cup), it's a short drive to the POLIN Museum in Warsaw where yesterday, on two hours' sleep, we received a whistle-stop tour of Jewish history in Poland and Central Europe. Did you know that, fleeing persecution in Western Europe, Jewish merchants first settled in Poland in the tenth century? That Polish coins minted in the twelfth century bear Hebraic markings? That by the sixteenth century almost three quarters of the world's Jewish population lived in Poland? That before the war one in ten Poles were Jews?[79]

From the museum, set within the borders of what was once the ghetto, it's a quick walk in the glassy morning sun to a small residential square, a courtyard in the shadow of two blocks of neat-looking flats, its 'open' side blocked by a twelve-foot brick wall. Morning commuters are pounding the cobbles with coffees in hand and somewhere in the trees birds are probably singing as we gather in a circle for our first education session of the day.

In 1939, just before the commencement of the war, the Jewish population of Warsaw, numbering 337,000, accounted for 29 per cent of the total population of the city. The Germans invaded on 31 August and by November 1939 they'd issued their first set of anti-Jewish decrees. All Jewish men, women and children over the age of ten were required to wear white armbands adorned with blue Stars of David. They were banned from train travel and their businesses marked by signs declaring their Jewishness. More explicit economic decrees soon followed,[80] quickly escalating into German seizure of Jewish enterprise.

On 12 October 1940, the establishment of a ghetto was announced; by November, housing 140,000 Jews, it was sealed off with a 3.5-metre-high wall topped with glass and barbed wire. The daily food ration for occupants of the ghetto was 180 calories, roughly a quarter of that allocated to non-Jewish Poles and around 8 per cent of the nutritional value of an official German ration book. This meant smuggling was essential. Usually it was practised

---

79 No. I knew none of this. And more.
80 Non-Jews were forced to obtain special permits before buying or leasing from Jewish businesses, effectively ending Jewish trade with the non-Jewish population.

by children who would remove loose bricks to scale the perimeter wall and on the other side barter for food with anything they could lay their hands on: jewellery, watches, pots and pans they'd secreted from workshops where they performed forced labour. The punishment for those caught? They were shot. (The memory of my seventeenth birthday, when I found out my girlfriend wasn't my girlfriend, is fading fast.)

Life continued like this for almost two years, schooling outlawed, public prayer banned, the death rate rising month on month before stabilising between the four to five thousand mark, until July 1942 when, directly following the completion of Treblinka, the Nazis announced their plans for 'Resettlement'. Already the Jews were accustomed to night raids where German police seized and shot inmates from a prepared list, but in accordance with Operation Reinhardt, the name given to the extermination of the Jews, the final leg of the Final Solution, the ghetto was liquidated. Jews were ordered to assemble with a maximum of 15 kg in luggage, three days of provisions and any valuables they might still possess. In July, 64,606 were sent to Treblinka. In August they were joined by around 135,000 more, although most of July's intake was already dead. The square we're standing in is the *Umschlagplatz*, where husbands and wives, parents and children assembled to wait for the freight trains. They didn't need rounding up; they thought there might be food.

Following the deportations, the remaining occupants of the ghetto, led by representatives of various youth movements, staged an uprising against the German soldiers and the self-selected Nazi-subordinate Jewish police, and the next part of our morning – it's not yet eight o'clock – is the Heroes' Walk, from the Umschlagplatz back to the museum square. Here, plaques and stones commemorate leaders of the resistance, both physical and spiritual, such as Mordechai Anielewicz, a youth movement principal who led a makeshift Jewish combat battalion, and Janusz Korczak, an educator and children's rights advocate who calmly led a line of children from the orphanage to their certain fates 'in clean clothes, as if for an outing on Shabbat'.[81] One stone that catches my attention is for Rabbi Kalonymus Kalman Shapira, whose reading of the Talmud granted Jews permission to suppress their religious identities. This, he taught, was different from the Inquisitions where Jews were ordered to convert or die; the Christians had wanted Jewish souls but the Nazis wanted only their bodies, and so every Jew had a duty to cover their roots if the opportunity arose.[82]

Then it's back on the bus for the three-hour drive to Lublin, from where my bubba and zeyde set out on their journey to the new world. We start our tour in the yeshiva, the centre of Jewish study, at one time the largest in Europe, and the one place in Lublin I can be fairly certain my ancestors never stepped foot inside, but from there it's the shortest drive yet to Majdanek, where almost certainly they did. One of six death camps built by the Nazis on Polish territory, Majdanek is the best preserved but least known about instrument of the Nazis' attempts to exterminate world Jewry – it would score well on *Pointless* but not on *Family Fortunes*. Set back not fifty metres from a main road on which traffic busily flows and in what was once farmland overlooked by the city (it's worth remembering that six million Poles died under German occupation, three million non-Jewish), this is the place where my direct family were most likely murdered.

Here, you're greeted by a large Soviet monument that looks exactly like nothing – it's less a memorial than a thirty-foot testament to Russian indomitability, a piece of propaganda – but everything else is pretty much as it once was. Today the gas chambers are

---

81 From the *Deportation Diary* of Wladyslaw Szlengel.
82 As in chess so in life: always do what your opponent least wants.

dressed in marquees, like shy bathers changing on a beach, as workers in khaki shorts perform some restorations. (Are they agency workers? On a week's contract?) This is a small mercy, a welcome filter, another reminder that we're here and not here, because here is a time not a place, but in the barracks it's easier to forget – harder to remember – that it's 2019, a full eight decades since the start of the war.

In the barracks we have our second discussion of the day, this time on capos, those Jewish inmates chosen to carry out punishments and select prisoners for work, whose wrath and whims could determine your chances of survival. Some were brutal, some kind, most both, but is it right to count them as survivors? Were they double victims or amoral opportunists: doomed men who knew their fates, and who understood that if not them it would be someone else? Or were they would-be turncoats who felt their end depended on their capacity for cruelty? We can't decide. There are raised voices and some tears. Two Jews, three opinions.

Then it's on to the crematoria where the bodies murdered by gas, gunfire or simply starvation were incinerated three at a time in ovens that unsurprisingly, but no less shockingly, look like ovens. Initially Majdanek was built as an internment camp with the gas chambers and crematoria added later during a mass expansion as it pivoted to genocide, but it's estimated that between 50,000 and 300,000 people were murdered here, not just Jews but French, Dutch, Soviet and Polish inmates, political prisoners and criminals from Germany, Austria and Italy. Still, the residents of Lublin had two years to accustom themselves to the camp's presence before its chimneys started billowing black smoke, but on 3 November 1943, following attempted escapes at Sobibor,[83] the Nazis put into effect

---

83 Another death camp.

Aktion Erntefest[84] in which 40,000 Jews, including 18,000 from Majdanek, were shot and buried in mass graves.

Leaving the crematoria, we're directed towards a monument set several metres back from a series of deep, zigzag-shaped trenches, which the Jews who were ordered to dig were told were for repelling Russian tanks. I'm sceptical of the value of imaginative empathy. The latter should be possible without the former. If you have to imagine it then is it really empathy? Also, with something this big and so removed from your personal experience, it seems crass, almost fetishistic. I'm also uncomfortable with privileging a personal connection to secure a sense of proximity since there's an obvious corollary here: without the connection, it matters less. But standing here, the city to my right, looking out across a skyline that offers few deictical markers, my eyes settle on a tree, leaning as if in italics. I have no idea how old or even what type of tree it is – Imogen would know – but nevertheless the thought is impossible to suppress: *This is the last thing they saw.*

When people asked me why I'd chosen to spend my thirty-fourth birthday on a tour of Nazi concentration camps I told them either that I had a book to finish or I was going so I didn't have to again. (Sometimes, if I knew them well, I told them it was Jewry duty.) But the real answer is less pithy and a lot more earnest. The tour we (my old comedy-writing partner, his sister, two more old friends and I) are on is called March of the Living and bills itself as an unforgettable educational journey that brings together participants from all round the world and culminates, on Yom Hashoah (Holocaust Memorial Day), in a triumphant march from Auschwitz to Birkenau. The real attraction for me, though, and I suspect for most of us, is the chance to spend some time with

---

84 Operation Harvest Festival.

survivors, who volunteer their time and in many cases their emotional well-being to accompany groups on tours of the camps, give testimony and answer what questions you might have. I've chosen to come this year because I believe in what Elie Wiesel says, that when you hear a witness you become a witness, and because who knows how much longer they'll be able to run these tours. Even the youngest survivors are now in their late eighties. Health problems prevent many from talking as often as they once did and within several years there'll be no survivors left; it may not be crueller but time is certainly more thorough than any murderous regime.

This is something that Jewish communities and charities like the Holocaust Educational Trust have been aware of and preparing for for a long time, but the truth is no one knows which way things will go. Like a song that after so long passes into the public domain, the Holocaust will soon be up for grabs. It's no surprise that deniers and revisionists have been emboldened as the number of survivors has dwindled and it seems unlikely that the testimony of second- (and third-) generation survivors will have the same impact on young people that first-hand accounts of the camps and ghettoes undoubtedly do, especially young people who are growing up mindful of the ways in which pictures and footage can be easily manipulated.[85] It's more important than ever, then, that we listen to the stories of survivors while we still have the chance lest the Holocaust, like climate change or transgenderism, become another partisan truth. All of us, but Jews more than most, have been cast as custodians to a memory we hold, at best, in the second or third person, and it's up to us to ensure it endures and that lessons are

---

85 As a young woman from India explained to me, when she first heard of Holocaust denial, despite understanding the agenda it came with, a part of her wanted to believe it; it seemed preferable to believing that the Holocaust was possible.

learned, even if the only real lesson is that man is capable of acts of staggering inhumanity.

But while hearing a witness might make you a witness, meeting a survivor does not make you a survivor, and it's impossible to ignore that there's something surreal about all this, that it's outside our comprehension, in direct contravention of our lived experience. I can only describe it thus: we're here and not here – there's a coordinate missing. And isn't there a limit to how far the imagination can (and should) take you?

Before we leave Majdanek, we gather under the dome of an enormous urn, maybe forty metres in diameter and piled so high with ashes it looks like a sand dune, as a rabbi says Kaddish, the Jewish prayer of mourning. While we're standing there the heavens open – there's no other way to say it – and at once all hundred of us are the directors of our own personal films. As rain slides down the roof and billows into ghosts I feel nothing at all besides the nagging suspicion that I've already reached my limit for how much this can move me, that this is too on the nose.

The next day is another early start as we leave Lublin and travel the hundred miles to Belzec. It's banal in the extreme to describe a death camp as chilling but Belzec is unusual (sadly not unique) among the Nazis' genocidal apparatus, offering as it does a glimpse of a little-known counter-history. Belzec is what the Holocaust looks like in a world where the Nazis succeeded in exterminating the Jews. By the end of 1941, 80 per cent of the victims of the Holocaust were still alive; by the end of 1942, 80 per cent were dead. This statistical inversion is largely down to camps like Belzec, which were built with the exclusive purpose of murdering Jews.[86]

---

86 I've since learned that a high proportion of Lublin's Jews were taken straight to Belzec, meaning it's more likely my family were murdered here than Majdanek.

The first 'experimental killings' were carried out in February 1942 by orders of the Nazi high command under the auspices of Operation Reinhardt. With train connections from Lvov, Stanislawow, Tarnow, Przemysl, Rzeszow and Krakow via the nearby Rawa Ruska railway centre, Belzec received transports from across Europe as towns and villages were decimated. By December, 450,000 Jews had been murdered. At first their bodies were buried in mass graves but soon, with the release of gases, the land became unstable and fluids began to leak down the hill towards the train line just fifty metres away. Jewish forced labourers, later murdered at Sobibor, were ordered to exhume the bodies and burn them on giant pyres made of railway sleepers. The bones were crushed and used as fertiliser. Already, prior to being murdered, the victims had been shaved so their hair could be used to stuff mattresses. (And it's Jews who get shit for being stingy.) Then, once its mission was complete, the Nazis dismantled the camp, ploughed over the land and built a farmhouse on top.

Today Belzec is a memorial, consisting of a museum filled with photos of victims, and a roughly-to-scale monument: an almost square area approximately the size of two ploughed football pitches separated by a pathway that leads between them to what transpires is a sheer granite wall. The path starts level with the ground but with each step the earth rises up on either side. There are only two known survivors of Belzec. One died the day he was due to give testimony but the other, Rudolf Reder, wrote a book – later corroborated by German and Polish testimonies – from which we know what we do of the camp's layout. It's unclear whether the path represents the 'Sluice' along which naked victims were driven with bayonets and knives to the gas chamber at its end, but neverthe-less, as the land continues to rise and the sky disappears until you're standing at the base of a twenty-foot cross-section of earth, regard-less of your stance on imaginative empathy, it's impossible not to feel your breathing constrict as panic winds around your chest. The power is in the increments. A moment ago you were above ground. No one step was decisive but now there's no escape. Once you've set off down the path there's nowhere to go but on. It's entirely possible this is the worst place on Earth.

At the end of the path, carved into the granite, is a quote attributed to Job: 'Earth, do not cover my blood; let there be no resting place for my outcry.' It's wrenching to read given the context – you're literally underground – but in its anguish it succeeds in expressing something often lost in my understanding of the Holocaust. We talk about the Jews as victims and lionise those who faced death with dignity, who went to their fates with their heads held high, reciting blessings and singing prayers, and we make jokes at our expense that appear to come from a place of at least grudging acceptance. But what part of this can you accept?

Later, in Auschwitz, we'll see the insides of a gas chamber[87] and some of us will reach out to touch the scratch marks in the brickwork. That the Nazis never faced justice for what they did to the Jews periodically fills me with both rage and despair, but what would justice look like for this? What does it mean in a world where the natural order has been so completely inverted, where mothers disavow babies since to do otherwise is to seal two fates?

Again we say Kaddish, this time led by a relative of victims, and light candles. This time there's no biblical storm to curate our emotions. On the walk back to the bus we pass the names of towns from which transports were sent. There are too many to list and many reoccur – when there was more than one transport. Most of the names I haven't heard of but I recognise some from a childhood watching the Champions League and the Cup Winners' Cup: Stuttgart, Dortmund . . .

---

87 I'll refine my view that Belzec is the worst place on Earth.

On the bus to Krakow we eat sandwiches and talk about football – that night Tottenham face Ajax in the first leg of the Champions League semi-final. Later I FaceTime Arthur and tell him about all the chocolate I'll be bringing home.

◆ ◆ ◆

In the novel I abandoned before writing this there was one section I was particularly proud of, in which the narrator recalled the run-up to and the day of his bar mitzvah. Like me, the narrator was a lapsed Jew with a non-Jewish partner, and like me had no vestigial belief in God or the cosmos. In the weeks preceding the ceremony he learned his portion from a tape with no curiosity about what the words meant and was forced to take a test that proved he understood its significance. Sitting in the oppressive warmth of his Sunday-school classroom, he vacillated on what to do. The bar mitzvah stood to land him a significant payday: recompense for all those missed Christmases and Friday nights in, but he couldn't proceed in good faith if he rejected the beliefs – the Jewishness – it was based on. The test was only one question long and required that he complete the sentence, *After my bar mitzvah I will be _____*. Eventually he cocked his pen and scratched four quick letters. *Rich*.

But afterwards, on the day of the ceremony, something strange happens. Standing in front of the congregation, at the pulpit or whatever it's called, his grandfather – an Auschwitz survivor – in the audience, he starts to recite the Hebrew words he's learned to recite. The rabbi has handed him a silver pointer so he can keep his place on the ornate scroll that is unrolled before him and he is pretending to do so, hopping the tip from word to word like a character in a platform game, when to his surprise he feels a tightening in his chest. It has something to do with reading – or pretending to read – from right to left, like you're moving backwards in time:

> *I looked down and realised to my shock that rather than the series of arbitrary scrawls they'd been just seconds ago, the letters before me made a kind of sense. What they were saying I wasn't sure – I only knew I was being addressed – and the impression was fleeting, like passing clouds conspiring to resemble a face, but for its duration I felt something I hadn't before and haven't since: the sudden knowledge, solid in its certainty, that I was part of something bigger than me . . . that I was experiencing something I'd always fail to explain.*

The first part of this story, the approach to the bar mitzvah test and the test in cheder, were taken from life but the second part, the revelation and sudden sense of connection, were fabrication. The day of my own bar mitzvah I played centre back for Radlett Rangers in the morning and in the afternoon watched Chelsea beat Bolton two–nil in the final game of the Premier League season (if we'd lost we'd have relegated Everton, who for some reason, perhaps that they also wear blue, I thought of as bitter rivals). In between I posed for photos and squirmed through the shortest Torah portion that luck could've allotted me. I didn't quite hate every minute – there was the moment at the end when I was pelted with sweets and threw one back, nailing my brother Daniel between the eyes – but I felt no more connected than our dial-up modem as I waited for my dad to conclude yet another work phone call. My bar mitzvah, as I'd seen it, was always my exit point. It was the final time I'd have to engage with being Jewish.

But twenty years later I did get a version of the moment I'd assigned to my literary avatar. I wasn't at the pulpit – it's called a *bima* – I was part of the congregation, and it was the first time I'd been so or even stepped inside a shul in more than fifteen years. The occasion was another bar mitzvah but it was one taking place under unusual circumstances. The bar mitzvah boy wasn't a becurtained thirteen-year-old but Zigi, my friend's grandfather and my erstwhile officemate. Zigi had never had a bar mitzvah since at the age he was due one he was in transit to Auschwitz, but such is the Jewish attitude to timekeeping that at eighty-three a window reopens. For most people this is the chance for a spiritual re-up, less a rite of passage than a second bookend, but for Zigi it was his first opportunity to become a man in the eyes of his community. In the audience were his two daughters, his six grandchildren and, on the lap of Darren's sister-in-law Claire, Jake, the first of his three great-grandsons.

I was running late and had been stopped at the door by a security man who didn't recognise me from my time as a congregant but I took my seat in time to see Zigi leave his.

It wasn't the same building where twenty years earlier I'd phoned in my portion and thrown sweets at my brother, and outside which I'd caused a terror alert by forgetting my games bag; it was a temporary structure next door since that shul was under reconstruction and because, like the rainstorm, that would've been too on the nose. But it didn't detract from the tightening in my chest: like a line that had been allowed to fall slack had been snapped suddenly taut. The realisation seems too obvious to call it an epiphany and too revelatory to call it anything else, but that day I understood that a religion was not a faith, that it need not point upwards. It could just as easily point backwards. Or sideways. It didn't have to mean something to mean something. It wasn't a tower, it was a bridge.

It feels like there ought to be a version of the Carnegie Hall joke for Auschwitz but in reality you just follow the signs from Krakow. Viktor Frankl, in *Man's Search for Meaning*, describes approaching Auschwitz: the 'dreadful realization', the train shunting as it neared the main station, how the 'very name stood for all that was horrible'. These days, though, if you didn't know better, you might be arriving at any other out-of-town tourist destination. As the roads slow and our bus leaders pause *Schindler's List* – the Nazis are in the middle of liquidating the ghetto – hotels start to appear on the roadside and the pavements sprout pizzerias offering lunch deals in English: free garlic bread with any order, buy one drink get one free. It's only in the car park that where you are hits you.

The first thing I can tell you about visiting Auschwitz is that to use the toilets you have to pay two zloty: no zloty, no potty. One of our guides tells us a story, possibly apocryphal, about a survivor who when told about the charge rolled up his sleeve and explained, 'The last time I was here we didn't have to pay.' The second thing I can tell you is that familiarity with the image of Birkenau, where we start our tour, won't prepare you for the terrible awe you feel on confrontation with it in real life. A train track passes through a gated archway into what looks at first like an endless expanse lined on either side with barbed wire and the outlines of barracks. Parts of this train line have been preserved and can be seen throughout the car park and the surrounding roads, and if traced backwards it would lead to the twenty-seven countries from which the Nazis exported Jews to be murdered here. As with Belzec, there's a horrible sense of inevitability, of things moving one way. The first rail was laid on 10 May 1933 with public burnings in Germany of books written by Jews, or earlier, in April, with the boycott of Jewish shops and businesses. Either way, this is where it all leads. It's like a plug has been pulled from the centre of the continent.

The next thing I can tell you is that it's not true that even the birds are silent but that silence, like everything, is cumulative, is the sum of absence, and deepens over time. From the gates we follow the train tracks to the disembarkation point between the men's and women's camps. This is where the first selections took place. Where parents were split from children, friends from friends, husbands from wives. Where women pricked their fingers to rouge their cheeks and preteens tried to age three years in an hour. For most, though – and it's important to remember this – the two lines weren't life and death but murder by gas or murder by starvation.

While exact figures are difficult to find, of the minimum 1.3 million people deported to Auschwitz between 1940 and 1945, more than 1.1 million are thought to have been murdered, not counting those who died on death marches when the camp was evacuated as the Russians drew near. On 27 January 1945, when Soviet forces entered the camp, they liberated just seven thousand remaining prisoners, most of them dying or severely ill. But for now, at least, survival depended on being sent to the right. We know about the selections, incidentally, not just from testimonies of survivors but from photographs taken by the SS. These photographs, the only pictures of the camp in operation, were for internal circulation, a way of reporting progress to superiors, but they were also documentation for the future histories of the thousand-year Reich; there's no suggestion the Nazis were anything but proud of what they were doing. Most of the adults know better than to confront the camera's gaze and so look like extras, but to see children staring questioningly – or, worse, trustingly – down the lens is to stare into the heart of something so evil it appears to stare back.

Those sent left, as everyone knows, went straight to the gas chambers, although often they had to wait their turn on the grass outside while previous transports were murdered then incinerated, but those sent right went to the 'Sauna' where they experienced a ritual death: being stripped of their remaining possessions and having their heads shaved so they were unrecognisable to any friends and family who weren't yet dead. Then they were issued with a number that would replace their name, at first on a strip of fabric they'd have to sew to their 'uniform', later in ink administered straight to the flesh. Here, as ever, the name of the game for the Nazis was refinement. At first prisoners were tattooed on the chest with a small iron punch into which the guard would have to laboriously slot the numbered metal teeth but it soon proved more efficient to use a single needle fastened to a penholder and with this the tattoo site moved to the left outer forearm.

These kinds of refinements are on show throughout Birkenau, from the extension of the train lines so that they were closer to the crematoria, to the constant experiments into the most efficient way to burn bodies in a three-person oven; the eventual conclusion was one fleshy and two emaciated, with children burned on separate pyres. Already Belzec seems a distant memory and Majdanek a month ago and the thought of another six hours here is enough to make you question your life choices.

It's in the Sauna that we first see suitcases and personal effects: items of clothing, photos of babies.

While we're sitting on the grass to the right of the area known as 'Canada', where confiscated property was piled high in several barns and SS men could enrich themselves by procuring choice pieces, I get a text from my editor at the *Independent* asking if I'm free to write about the latest rumblings of scandal in Labour.[88] I text back that I can't write about anti-Semitism because I'm in Birkenau.

Then it's into a barracks to hear the testimony of a former inmate, Renee Salt, who incredibly, in her ninetieth year, is accompanying groups on every leg of this trip. I've heard survivors speak in the past but I've never seen anything like the courage required to willingly walk back through the gates of hell to warn others of its existence. There have been many times in my life that I've resented the choice I made to be a writer – that pact to be one-removed, on record but never quite present – but never have I felt more grateful for the shield of a notepad and pen than during the forty minutes I sat cross-legged, with a hundred other people, at Renee's feet listening to her tell her story.

I took copious notes, more in forty minutes than I took throughout the rest of the trip, but I'm not sure of the benefits of reproducing them here, of trying to summarise her story. To hear a witness, if you believe Elie Wiesel, is to become a witness, but

---

88 Jeremy Corbyn has written a foreword to a twentieth-century economics text that talks about a 'central ganglion of international capitalism . . . controlled chiefly by men of a single and peculiar race, who have behind them many centuries of financial experience'. Again, the foreword, which praises the book and ignores the anti-Semitism, doesn't *prove* Corbyn's an anti-Semite but demonstrates once more his yawning blind spot: that he doesn't recognise anti-Semitism, or if he does doesn't consider it disqualifying. Though, in the interests of balance, neither do Boris Johnson or Theresa May, who in the run-up to the 2019 General Election, to little public outcry, proudly unveiled a statue of the Conservative MP Nancy Astor, a Nazi sympathiser who viewed Hitler as a solution to the global problem of Jewish-backed communism, described Jews as 'Christ killers' in a letter that dismissed the Holocaust as 'a rough time', and blamed anti-Semitism on something intrinsically unlikable in Jewish nature.

these things have a half-life; you don't become a witness by hearing someone who grew up in the Home Counties during the birth of Britpop, whose deepest trauma was the critical response to the third Limp Bizkit album, tell you about the horrors of Auschwitz. And why should Renee's tragedy and trauma be folded into my own narrative? At shivas, the week of mourning that follows a Jewish funeral, the family are required to cover all the mirrors in their household because death is no respecter of vanity and in its shadow it's crass to think of oneself. Invariably this fails since what is mourning if it isn't personal. But the Holocaust is different. Maybe it's the scale, maybe it's the absurdity, or maybe it's just that it's so far removed from most people's experience – so far outside of our intellectual and imaginative capacities – but more than anything what I felt in Birkenau (and later in Auschwitz) was an overwhelming sense – complicated by everything this book's been about, by the *there but for the grace of God* – that this wasn't about me.[89]

And at the same time, so much of my sense of self, so much of how I understand my life, is predicated on what happened here. Passing under the gates of Auschwitz, under the jauntily set, almost Comic Sans, *Arbeit Macht Frei*, something strange takes place. When people go to Paris they take pictures of themselves with the Eiffel Tower or the Sacré-Coeur, never just the monuments on their own. I believe they do this to prove that they exist: not the buildings, but them. *Us.* People take pictures of themselves under the gate at Auschwitz too and it's hard not to think there's a similar instinct at play. Auschwitz is so (I feel queasy saying this) iconic that you don't expect to ever see it in real life. Being there makes you feel actual, grounds you in time, offers a mirror by which to authenticate your existence, but ironically it's the place – not you – that feels unreal.

89 You can watch Renee's testimony online and I would urge you to do so.

Compared to Birkenau, with its open expanses and its half-collapsed chimney stacks, it feels like a film set, like it's been curated. Partly that's because it has. Auschwitz is now a museum that attracts over a million visitors a year and is frequently recognised for its educational programmes. But there's something else too. Something that's harder to explain.

If you go to the Catacombs or to Checkpoint Charlie you're grounded in history, but in Auschwitz there's a feeling like you're standing outside of it. Whether the Holocaust is unique is a debate that achieves very little, a question of scale not an argument of category, but Auschwitz can stake a reasonable claim to represent the zenith of man's capacity for cruelty. It's not the exception that proves the rule but the exemplification of a rule that runs counter to everything we suppose about progress, decency, justice[90] and humanity. Auschwitz is an island unto itself. A universe of cruelty.

While in Birkenau it's the immediacy that hits you, the untouchedness and the sum of absences; in Auschwitz it's the accumulation of small details. All visitors to Auschwitz, whether individuals or part of a group, are required to take a guided tour. Even our witnesses must don headphones and keep their thoughts to themselves as a Polish woman who looks like Rose Byrne's sadder younger sister, whose job it is to do this twice a day, walks us through the mechanics of an attempted extermination. Her affectless delivery, flat as a reservoir, so different to the tones in which our educators have cajoled us to debate amongst ourselves, at first seems jarring, but quickly it becomes clear that it's the only suitable conduit for the delivery of the information it's her job to impart – not least for her mental health. Here's where the first mass exterminations took

---

90   Roughly 15 per cent of the SS who worked in Auschwitz were prosecuted.

place;[91] here's where a thousand people slept, ten to a bunk; here's where children were taken for experimentation; here's where prisoners were tortured and those who attempted to escape were suffocated to death in windowless cells; here's where the commandants lived and their families played; here's where those who were too sick for the gas chambers were shot in the head.

There are tall green trees, stirred by a cooling breeze, and the sun drips through them. It's a beautiful day. It helps to think of it as a picture in negative, the present read from right to left. The orchestra the prisoners march past every morning on their way to work and march back past, in smaller numbers, on their return at night isn't an orchestra and what they're playing isn't music. It's another selection. Fall out of time and that's exactly where you'll be.

Viktor Frankl, who detailed his experiences in Auschwitz in the first half of *Man's Search for Meaning*, in his future career as a pioneer of logotherapy talked a lot about hyperintention: the paradox that the more you will something (sleep, dry armpits, an erection), the more elusive it becomes. Auschwitz for all of us is the place on this tour we've imagined our reactions to most and I can't have been the only one suffering from the anxiety that it wouldn't move me as much as I expected. This anxiety is quickly revealed as precisely the sort of myopic narcissism that being in Auschwitz renders mute, but past a point it's just too much; the body retreats into safe mode. Our capacity for grief is not infinite and there's only so many piles of shoes, suitcases with names on them (the *hope*) and rugs woven from human hair you can see before you start to feel numb.

But that's where being a parent comes in. It's one thing to feel numb for yourself – and to question the benefits of imaginative empathy – but it's quite another to see an outfit in a case that you might dress your son in or a pair of shoes he'd have now

91 Nine hundred people in Block 11 in September 1941.

outgrown and not feel that line snap taut. In one block, curated by Yad Vashem, the Israeli Holocaust museum, there's an exhibition of artworks discovered on barrack walls. Children's drawings. There are pictures of men with guns, tanks, gallows, animals in cages, bodies piled on the ground, one where the gates of Birkenau look like the mouth of a monster sucking in trains through the rail that issues from it like a straw. But then there are pictures of birds, of children skipping, of a mother with a pram, of trees – they look like birch. Also in this block, colourised and set to piano, projected on the walls is footage of Jews from across Europe in the 1920s and '30s. Skiing. Smiling. Getting married. Jumping off jetties. They look happy, alive, some playing up to the camera, some a little stiff in front of it. They look like families.

◆ ◆ ◆

Our tour ends in a gas chamber.

◆ ◆ ◆

On the drive back to our hotel we're briefed about the march the next day. For many people, this march, a triumphant walk out of Auschwitz and the mile or so to Birkenau where there'll be a ceremony for Yom Hashoah, the international day of Holocaust remembrance, is the point of the trip but for me, at best, it's an afterthought. This, we're told, is the one day a year when Auschwitz doesn't look like Auschwitz. There are ten thousand people from all over the world who come together to commemorate the Holocaust. It's a political event, we're warned, and there's much about it that might make us uncomfortable, but we're urged, where possible, to keep an open mind.

There is, in my view, no unifying message to be taken from the Holocaust, certainly not one that can be easily distilled into a political stance. Throughout the week, in small numbers, I've seen Israeli flags and while intellectually I understand the connection, they've made me uncomfortable in a way that's complicated but also isn't. So far, no one's talked to me about Israel or my views on the current government's actions, and most of us are young and left-leaning, the kind of people likely to share my discomfort, but I'm anxious. Is this a memorial or a rally? More to the point, am I going to make this about myself? Am I going to have a fight in Auschwitz? I'm so used to being the only Jew in the conversation – my identity is built on it – and it's been a long time since I've been in a roomful, and I've certainly never been in a crowd of ten thousand. Will my natural contrariness kick in? Will it cheapen an experience that has the potential to be hugely powerful and maybe offer something in the way of redemption?

True enough, Auschwitz doesn't look like Auschwitz. It looks like Wembley Way or T in the Park or anywhere else that large crowds assemble. People are waving flags – Argentina, South Korea, France, Hungary, even Japan. We're dressed in matching blue jackets. There are banks of Portaloos and lines stretching back from them. No zloty, some potty.

We're given packed lunches and told it's up to us what we do with them. If we want to wait for the walk between camps to eat then we should, but equally if we're comfortable eating sandwiches inside a concentration camp we shouldn't let others' reticence stop us. There's no right way to act. No official line on whether we're commemorating or celebrating. People are hugging hello and taking selfies with each other. Someone's brought a guitar. Representatives from different delegations are swapping badges and lanyards. There's an unofficial competition to see who can amass the most. My friend's sister, Zigi's grand-daughter, ends up looking like Jennifer Aniston's character in *Office Space*, or more like her boss who insists fifteen pieces is the minimum *flair*. To say *to say it's surreal is an understatement* is an understatement.

Outside one of the blocks, one we didn't visit yesterday, I get talking to Ola, our Polish educator. She seems ill at ease and a little put out and tells me about another game, one of her own devising: Spot the Pole. Generally you can tell by the look of mortification writ large on their faces. Ola is a genealogist and a PhD candidate whose focus of study is the history of Jews in Poland. We haven't spoken before but on our first night in Poland she shared her story with the group. Only *story* isn't quite the right word since a story is only a story when it's finished and Ola's exploration of her Jewish identity is very much ongoing.

Ola grew up not knowing she was Jewish, believing instead, like many Poles whose parents had grown up under communism (when no one had the right of religious expression), that she had 'Jewish roots'. She knew her grandparents were Jewish and that her mum had these Jewish roots too but she grew up in a secular home. 'The only difference between me and my Catholic friends was that I was never baptised and at Christmas we went skiing.' She thought Jews were always religious and that to be one you needed both your parents to be, and it wasn't until her thirties when she went to Sweden on a training programme for people who work in Jewish organisations that the question of her own Jewishness crystallised. Away from home and the assumptions she'd held, the option presented itself: she was Jewish too – if she wanted to be. Her mum had always lit candles but without any blessings and she talked about Jewish history, and it was Ola's job, she decided, to fill in the practice. She was still too shy to go to shul but the next year she approached a rabbi and told him she wanted a bat mitzvah, which was the beginning of an immersion in the traditions and customs. Everything that the war then communism had taken away. She started going to shul, first tentatively then weekly. 'I felt education about [being] Polish isn't enough, I have more obligation towards our community.'

There are some questions I've been wanting to ask Ola. Some annoying journalistic ones about her family's past to help me clarify the timelines but also one I wanted to ask the other night on a visit to a Jewish community centre in Krakow, where one of those young, cool rabbis I'm innately mistrustful of gave a talk about a revival of Jewish life in Poland. This centre, opened by Prince Charles in 2008, was run by non-Jewish volunteers and I could see that in the context in which it existed it was crucial to fostering a sense of community and provided a necessary beacon for other Jews who wanted to explore their identities. But even here, where a Jewish community centre is the ultimate sign of rebellion and defiance – the ultimate *fuck you* – I found myself squirming in my seat as talk moved to a new Jewish pre-school the centre was hoping to open.

My question, which I hadn't had the nerve to ask the rabbi – I couldn't find a way to word it that in the circumstances wouldn't have sounded confrontational – was about the word *community*. How central was congregating, of communing if not with God then with one another, to the maintenance of Jewishness? Because it's taken me a long time but I feel secure in my Jewishness, and not only does it not require being around other Jews, it actively shrivels at the contact. Did this, in his eyes, make me a lesser Jew? Or was my version of Jewishness just as sustainable, possibly more so since if we continued to define ourselves in opposition to the outside world, even with frequent reminders that it is hostile to us, then hadn't we lost? Whereas if each Jew cultivated their own version of Jewishness, didn't we have a better shot at plurality, which is a better word than *assimilation* since it understands that there is no one thing to assimilate to, and allows for the possibility that nothing is lost?

I didn't know what I'd wanted from asking this question – reassurance, absolution, or just to play devil's advocate. But for whatever reason I hadn't been able to ask this the other night at the Jewish community centre in front of a roomful of people where Ola was sitting in front of me, nodding along. Before I have the chance to ask it now, Ola answers it for me. We're talking about going to shul on a Saturday morning when she stops and sighs. Adjusts her glasses and pushes some hair up her head. 'You know, honestly, there are some Saturdays it's the last thing I want to do. If I didn't have to I probably wouldn't. I'd stay in bed reading or have brunch with my sister.' She goes on: 'If I lived somewhere like the UK I'd probably be super lapsed. I'd probably never go to shul. I wouldn't do anything. I wouldn't even keep kosher. You know?'

It's embarrassing how, often, little's needed to prompt an epiphany. How had I failed to see that my version of Jewishness, the fact I was free to decide what bits were important, came from a position of great privilege? That it was built on the security of knowing there was a community to reject.

All around us people from various continents are still exchanging badges and greetings in whatever lingua francas they can muster and we continue talking while we wait for the march to begin – Jewish timekeeping sticking to tradition. Eventually the march does start, though it's really more of a shuffle, and Ola and I drift apart in the crowd. But at some point later, on the road between Auschwitz and Birkenau, we bump into each other again and resume talking. About our childhoods, our families. The differences between London and Warsaw. It's enough to keep us from considering the immediate context, to carry us through the gates of Birkenau to the stage, backed by a giant screen that's been set up between two crematoria. Here Ola's discomfort sharpens and we take a seat away to the side of the bleachers, away from the speakers, with our backs to the stage so we're facing the marquee that's been set up for survivors. It's another beautiful day, low twenties, and I'm regretting the decision not to pack my trusted factor 50 – like Woody, I don't tan, I stroke – and maybe it's this that bumps the conversation on to the subject of comedy.

'Do you know Larry David?'

'Of course! He's one of my heroes.' (I don't quite use the word *idol*.)

'I've got such a crush on him! I know he's too old for me but if he came up to me right now and asked me to marry him, I'd probably say yes.'

A ripple of unease runs through the crowd; someone (the US ambassador?) has mentioned Donald Trump and his support for Israel. Ola and I both tense. We let the feeling roll across us, dragging a surf of mild nausea, then go back to listing our favourite episodes of *Curb*. The one where Larry has to pretend to be *frum* to befriend a city official. His argument with Michael J. Fox. The one where he compliments the host of a party on the size of his prepubescent son's penis. The topper: his response when asked by Cheryl why he would do this. He'd taken a risk.

A few months earlier I'd sat on my grandparents' sofa in Middlesex. It took several hours to extract their life stories, at the end of which I asked the question I realised only then that all along I'd been building towards. There's an old Jewish joke about a kid coming home from school and telling his mum he's been cast in the class play as the husband, to which the mum consoles him, 'Next year, you'll get a speaking part', but my grandparents answered in unison and without hesitation. Is my son Jewish?

'Of course, he's our family.'

On stage a survivor with terminal cancer is giving testimony and perhaps in part it's the guilt that my back is turned . . . and even now, after thirty-five years, after two hundred pages, I'm still not certain I know what it means, but I've never felt more Jewish.

Afterword
(January 2020)

On 13 December 2019, Britain woke up, or went to bed, to the news that Jeremy Corbyn's Labour party had been defeated in the General Election it had been coaxed into calling for, and the prospect of another five, probably ten, years of Tory rule under a prime minister whose exclusionary outlook and casually nativist rhetoric have powered careers first in journalism then politics; a man who, in response to the Macpherson Report following the death of Stephen Lawrence, called discrimination on racial grounds as 'natural as sewage'. Some, including those on the left, such as ex-London mayor Ken Livingstone, who by two a.m. had conjured the monolithic bogeyman of a 'Jewish vote', saw the result as a rejection of Corbyn and an indictment of his reputation, whether earned or inflated, as compromised on anti-Semitism. Sajid Javid, Johnson's chancellor of the exchequer, declared the day a bad one for anti-Semites – and, by extension, a good day for Jews.

If this were true it didn't account for the anti-Semitism charges that had tarred the government in the last month of its campaign, albeit to less media outcry (mud sticks more readily to a party founded on the principle of anti-racism than one founded on fiscal conservatism and distrust of immigrants), and that in the hours and days after the count continued to trickle through.

Nor did it demonstrate a realistic understanding of how highly or otherwise people privilege Jewish pain, or – more urgently – of how nationalism works. Among the Tories' manifesto promises, along with Getting Brexit Done and introducing a 'firmer and fairer' Australian-style points-based immigration system, was a pledge to give police new powers to arrest and seize the property of Gypsy, Roma and Traveller communities whose encampments are deemed unauthorised. State seizure of a community's possessions and the threat of incarceration is past the point of a slippery slope. Jews understand as well as anyone that an attack on one minority is an attack on us all.

The day before the election, mostly lost in the swirl of evasions and disinformation, two far-right gunmen opened fire on a kosher market in Jersey City. In response to the attack, which killed two members of the Orthodox community, Donald Trump issued an executive order, extending Jews protection under Title VI of the Civil Rights Act, which outlaws discrimination (in federal programmes) against racial or national groups. In signing this order, even in ostensible defence of a community under attack, effectively Trump codified the dual-loyalty trope that sees Jews as apart not a part of a host society, a trope that has tarred Jewish citizens since our first expulsions and resettlements.

On 30 December, Jews in Britain woke to the news that in Monsey, New York, five Jews had been wounded by a man wielding a machete as they celebrated the last night of Chanukah in the home of their rabbi, while in Hampstead, just a few streets from where, as teenagers, my friends and I mostly failed to get served, shops, cafés and a synagogue had been daubed with graffiti blaming Jews for 9/11. Some have claimed that the 9.11 that featured under the six-sided star is a reference to Kristallnacht, which took place on

9 November 1938, but this only demonstrates that when it comes to opposing anti-Semitism some are more interested in shifting the blame than standing with Jews; an allusion to Kristallnacht would suggest a far-right offender, but the sobering truth is there's no way of knowing for certain the culprit's political persuasion. It's worth reflecting on that.

Jewish identity, as I hope this book begins to convey, is complicated and the times we live in are confusing and will only continue to get more confusing. In this new political reality, which is not a moment of madness or a *Dallas*-style dream that we'll soon bemusedly wake up from, the truth is always partisan and no one is ever entirely secure. Now more than ever we must remember the value of solidarity. This solidarity must not be conditional on a group's perceived worthiness or on who, cynically, speaks up on its behalf, and must not be coloured by ancient antipathies that are written into lore and exploited by those who seek to control us through division. This is true of Jews and for Jews. We can and must acknowledge the individual nature of anti-Semitism while realising that *never again* means not ever for anyone: not the Roma of Italy, the subject of a proposed census by the coalition's populist Interior Ministry; not the Yazidi, massacred by ISIL and dispersed across the globe; and not for Uyghur Muslims, a million of whom, at the time of writing, are believed to be interned in Chinese re-education camps. Recognising persecution and standing shoulder to shoulder with those who are oppressed and dispossessed is a key part of what it means to be Jewish. The Holocaust should never be reduced to a teachable moment, and many who try have motives for doing so, but neither should it stand outside of history, all alone as a monument to itself, to its own irreducibility. Its irreplicability.

But what do I know? Two Jews, three opinions, and it's not only Jews who get to have an opinion. Ultimately there's only one part of Jewish experience that I'm qualified to speak to: my own.

For my part I'll continue to identify as Jewish with a small *J* and a big *ish*, to avoid synagogues and community centres and anything that even smells like a prayer – but to feel bad every morning when I make my porridge with oat milk since it's against the laws of kashrut to cook a kid in the milk of its mother. And when my son asks me, as I'm sure one day he will, that's what I'll tell him: that he's Jew*ish*.

Because the *ish*, I think, is where the truth resides. In an age of weaponised identity, where we're far more interested in our differences than in what unites us and where our politics sets us against each other in ever-smaller subgroups, we'd do well to remember that most things are fluid, that there's an *ish* in everything. As a Jew I'm as quick to forget this as anyone. We need to find a way to unite around our common humanity without erasing or downplaying the particularities of any group's experience. If we're to confront the challenges that face us as a species and triumph over those who seek to divide and deceive us, we need to realise we're all in this together. The question of Jewishness is a good place to start. We're not all Jews but we're all Jew-ish.

ENDNOTE

ⁱ Feel free to skip this but whether or not you believe he is seems to depend on whether you believe that having said anti-Semitic things makes you an anti-Semite. This might sound ironic but I mean it sincerely. It's true that Corbyn is a lifelong anti-racist campaigner and it's also true that he's often fallen short of condemning anti-Semitism in adequate terms. (His favourite formulation when issuing condemnations, '. . . anti-Semitism and all forms of racism', distances it from 'real racism' while obfuscating the issue – Labour has not been accused of being institutionally racist against any other minorities. It also refuses to acknowledge the particular nature of anti-Semitism that makes it so prevalent across political divides.) It's also true that he's angered many with his conciliatory language towards anti-Jewish organisations like Hamas and Hezbollah, but if I counted everyone I called 'friend' as a friend my birthday parties would be much better attended (although inviting for tea on the Commons terrace a man convicted of inciting anti-Jewish violence who has previously claimed that Jews bake bread with the blood of non-Jewish children – a rehashing of the ancient blood libel – does suggest some slightly warped judgement). But some comments he's made have been unquestionable – and indefensible – in their anti-Semitic effect. The one I can't look past is his claim to a London conference on the

Palestinian Right of Return in 2013 that Zionists in attendance, 'having lived in this country a very long time . . . some of them all their lives, don't understand English irony'. Typing this, I'm reminded of a conversation between Jerry and Kramer in *Seinfeld* when Jerry suspects their dentist, Tim Whatley, of converting to Judaism not for the religion but for the jokes. Kramer: 'And this offends you as a Jew?' Jerry: 'No, it offends me as a comedian!' In this case, though, I'm offended as both, but primarily as a Jew. The amount of othering packed into this short utterance is alarming. First, there's 'having lived in this country all their lives', which encodes so much about the possible limits to our integration. As Shami Chakrabarti wrote in her 2016 report on anti-Semitism for which Corbyn granted her a peerage: 'I have heard testimony and heard for myself first-hand the way in which the word "Zionist" has been used personally, abusively, or as a euphemism for Jew.' To imply that 'Zionists', be they Jews or not, are somehow not English, or need lessons in English values (in irony, no less, as if the English invented being in two places at once), despite having 'lived here all their lives' is ugly and exclusionary, and through its associations (why say *English* irony if you're talking about *English* Zionists?) anti-Semitic. Does having said this make him an anti-Semite? It makes him the speaker of an anti-Semitic utterance. But the emphasis on the distinction between these two statements is, again, problematic. If a woman reports sexism, you listen. If a black person reports racism, you listen. You don't double-down and insist they consider your intent. Racism is not inconsequential. Its intent, then, matters far less than its effect. This was one of several statements that hurt Jews.

ACKNOWLEDGMENTS

Thank you: to Nat Singer, Helen Singer and Zigi Shipper for lending your stories, to Olinka Sajdak and Daniel Greene for your insight and expertise, to Katherine Fry for your questions and suggestions, to Victoria Pepe for your faith and support, to Gordon Wise for your guidance and patience, and to my family, immediate and extended, who have contributed to this book in myriad ways. Finally, thank you to Imogen Haines, and to Arthur Greene, without whom this book wouldn't have been written and in half of the time.

Thank you also to every writer whose work I've cited and many I haven't. This book was never intended as a compendium of anti-Semitic incidents and in writing some sections I relied on the reporting of several campaigners who have compiled them more exhaustively and at greater cost to their mental health. These include Sara Gibbs, Marlon Solomon and Adam Wagner, all of whom can and should be followed on Twitter if you want to know more about allegations within the Labour party that led to the Jewish Labour Movement's 2019 submission to the Equality and Human Rights Commission.

Finally, thank you to the Society of Authors who, indirectly, by providing a grant for the novel this book once was, funded its completion, and who have now saved my career twice.

ABOUT THE AUTHOR

Photo © 2020 Imogen Haines

Matt Greene is an author, journalist, former screenwriter, and stay-at-home dad. He won a Betty Trask Award for his first novel, *Ostrich*. He teaches critical and creative writing in South London, where he lives with his partner and son. Find him on Twitter @arealmattgreene.